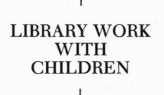

LIBRARY WORK
WITH
CHILDREN

Dorothy M. Broderick

LIBRARY WORK
WITH
CHILDREN

THE H. W. WILSON COMPANY • NEW YORK • 1977

ACKNOWLEDGMENTS

The poem "Truth" by May Sarton, which appears on pages 9 and 10 of this book, was first published in *Land of Silence and Other Poems* (1953) and is reprinted here by kind permission of Russell & Volkening, Inc., New York, New York 10017, as agents for the author.

The poem "Lies" by Yevgeny Yevtushenko, which appears on page 9 of this book, was first published in *Selected Poems of Yevtushenko* (1963) and is reprinted here by kind permission of the publishers, Pergamon Press, Inc., Elmsford, New York 10523.

Library of Congress Cataloging in Publication Data
Broderick, Dorothy M
    Library work with children.
    Bibliography: p.
    Includes index.
    1. Libraries, Children's. I. Title.
Z718.1.B82   027.62'5   77-14288
ISBN 0-8242-0620-7

FOR MARY K. CHELTON

Preface

THIS BOOK began as a revision of *An Introduction to Children's Work in Public Libraries* (1965). When I agreed to undertake a revision, I felt it would be merely a matter of updating titles and removing the sexist language of the original volume.

I had not read the original book since its publication; I had dipped into it occasionally for a quote, but mostly I encountered it in student papers, sometimes quoted directly and sometimes paraphrased just short of plagiarism. You can imagine my discomfort when I took sharp issue with a student, only to be told the views were my own.

So there came about a new beginning. A book developed from scratch, and this is it.

There are no answers in this book. There are some statements of fact. There are many opinions. Some of the opinions either are, or appear to be, contradictory. If these contradictions did not exist, there might be some answers. I am not uncomfortable with these contradictions, but some readers may be. I have tried to write a book that identifies issues and will force readers to make up their own minds about where they stand. People who want to be told what to think will not be happy with the pages that follow.

Many of the facts surrounding the issues presented have changed during the course of the writing, and may well change again between the time the manuscript goes to the printer and the book appears. For example, when I started writing the book, the Children's Services Division had gone on record with a statement on reevaluation of children's books; then it revised that statement; finally it rescinded the revised statement. Whatever the present CSD policy is, the issues leading to the original statement and its ultimate rescinding will not have gone away. In using the book, readers are asked to update the issues by researching developments occurring after June 1, 1977. Indeed, as this book is being made ready for press, the Children's Services Division has changed its name to the Association for Library Services to Children.

I would like to thank Gwen Creelman and Christopher Siefried, my graduate assistants at the Dalhousie School of Library Service, for the meticulous care with which they researched elusive pieces of information. Any bibliographic mistakes are mine, not theirs.

Bruce Carrick, my editor, has been magnificent both in human understanding and editorial skill and deserves a special thank you.

Finally, a pat on the head for Heidi-dog, and a scratch behind the ears for Billy-cat, without whom the book would have been finished sooner, but life would have been less enjoyable.

Dorothy M. Broderick
Ossining, New York

Contents

PART ONE:

The Collection

CHAPTER
ONE

Building a Library Collection

MOST CHILDREN'S librarians spend more time on the selection of materials than on any other professional activity—and with fewer results to show for it except crowded shelves. We read thousands of media reviews annually; spend countless hours previewing films, filmstrips, slides, recordings; and scan hundreds of books. Yet the end result of all this work can rarely be termed "a library collection." What we usually end up with is an unsystematic gathering of materials that we like to *think* of as a library collection.

What is our problem?

Very early in our professional training we are taught that it is knowledge of individual titles that will make us good librarians. Many library school courses in children's literature stress the number of books the students must read. Teachers often grade students by the number of books they have read, films they have viewed, or illustrators whose work they can identify.

This kind of training lays the groundwork for later professional behavior. At library conferences, after we have exchanged greetings, the chances are the first question we ask another librarian is, "Have you read. . . ?" or "What did you think of. . . ?" We talk continually about individual titles but very little about building a library collection.

One effect of this emphasis on individual titles is that we tend to feel guilty if we have not bought the current year's award-winning children's books, even if we do not need another fantasy title or another folktale in picture-book format. Another effect is

3

that we tend to read book reviews in isolation, selecting titles that carry strong recommendations but without relating their subject matter to our collection's needs.

In other words, we select titles but fail to build collections.

Why do we so often fail?

A large part of the problem is caused by fuzzy terminology. We talk about having a "materials selection policy" and we talk about "selection standards," but somewhere in the process of using the word "selection" in two different contexts, we blur the entire procedure.

What we need to talk about are two distinct—but related—matters: the collection policy and selection standards.

In order to build a library collection, we need a policy that defines the areas in which the library will conscientiously add materials. The collection policy defines not only these areas but also the content and even the format of the materials to be added. Good collection policies avoid generalities whenever possible and focus on specifics. Some examples of collection policy statements are:

1. All works by local authors and illustrators will be purchased.

2. No books by denominational presses will be purchased.

3. All books, historical or modern, with setting in (name of town, city, state, province) will be purchased.

4. All multiple copies of popular titles will be bought only in paperback editions.

5. No film will be purchased unless its content falls within a category established by this policy.

These collection-policy statements provide very specific guidelines as to the nature and the scope of the collection. When the words "all" or "no" are used, selection standards do not apply. There are, however, collection-policy statements that do require application of selection standards:

1. The poetry collection will contain a balance between anthologies and volumes by individual poets.

2. The collection will contain as many viewpoints as are available on all subjects added to the collection.

4

The last two statements require judgment for implementation. They are the ones that cause trouble. We will be discussing the exercise of judgment often in the course of this book.

In contrast to collection policy statements, selection standards can also be phrased as follows:

1. Materials should be appropriate to the age group for which they are intended.

2. Picture books whose purpose is to convey some concept (such as an understanding of color, number, or the alphabet) should be imaginative and well-designed.

Most librarians (outside of special libraries with their narrowly-defined clientele) operate under some sort of collection policy, even if it is vague and often unstated. But in matters of collection-building, vague assumptions can cause trouble. Assumptions cannot be passed on with much clarity or coherence to a new librarian, and so the "policy" is apt to change abruptly or disappear when the old librarian changes jobs or retires. In the meantime, the absence of a stated policy can lead to a distorted collection.

The mere presence of a collection policy will not help us ward off attempts by individual citizens or groups to impose restrictions on a library's collection. Censors do not care whether we have a policy or not. There is enough evidence in library literature to show that when a library must fight against censorship, community support is more important than the wording of a written policy.[1]

On the other hand, one way to build that community support is to develop the collection policy with representatives of the community as active participants. Every major group in the community—the P.T.A., the Chamber of Commerce, the League of Women Voters, NOW, the NAACP, to name just a few— should be asked to appoint a representative to the Collection Policy Committee. It can be argued that this will produce a large, unwieldy committee, but if we use our group dynamic skills well size should not be a problem. The establishment of subcommittees, with responsibility for certain topics, will keep the number of people actually involved small enough to guarantee smooth functioning. For example, sex education materials are a constant source of trouble from would-be censors. The time to let the various groups in the community fight out their different conceptions of what ought to be on the shelves is during the development of a collection policy and not in title-by-title attacks after the selections have been made.

For instance, it might prove beneficial for the Concerned Parents representative to hear first-hand from the Public Health Department's representative about the nature of the sexual problems being experienced by the community's youth.

I am not suggesting that a group like the Concerned Parents will change its point of view completely after participating in such a discussion. Clearly, however, a collection policy statement on sex-education materials that carries the approval of groups like the Public Health Department or the Association of Public Health Nurses will carry more weight with the community than one developed solely by librarians.

Involving the community in this process does not mean that the library staff relinquishes its professional responsibilities. What it does mean is that the librarians will be fulfilling their responsibility to educate the public in the complexities of building a library collection. For example, the statement that the library will purchase as many viewpoints as are available on a subject provides us with the opportunity to educate members of the community in the complexities of intellectual freedom. Most adults do not spend much time pondering the limits of free access to information. In fact, most adults in our society do not want children exposed to a wide range of ideas and attitudes. They prefer that all materials children encounter reflect their own value system. On this score, the only difference between liberal and conservative parents is in the content of the material they want their children to receive: atheistic parents can be just as upset when their children bring home books with a religious message as religious parents are when they see books they consider anti-religious in the hands of their children. Therefore, the development of a collection policy becomes vitally important because it will demonstrate to those involved the diversity of views held by members of the community. It will be more difficult for any participant to act as though his or her views were the only ones worth having in the library collection.

An additional benefit of this group process is that it allows us to identify experts in the community who can review materials for us in advance of purchase and who will thus be in a position to support our selection should an attack arise.

Before we undertake to work with members of the community in the development of a collection policy, we must have acquired at least some of the skills of a counselor, especially the art of active listening. We must be open enough to let the policy actually reflect the community's feelings and not to approach the development process with inflexible ideas of what the final document should be.

BALANCING THE COLLECTION

The myth of the balanced collection in a children's department needs to be dispelled once and for all. The range of attitudes available within children's books is considerably narrower than within adult books. Why? Because juvenile publishing is so sensitively attuned to changes in societal attitudes. As long as black people were considered quaint and curious creatures, that image was reinforced by most children's books. Only after both black and white people began to question and reject the old stereotypes and to demand books that depicted blacks as strong, dignified human beings, did juvenile publishing respond—perhaps not as rapidly as some would have liked, and too rapidly for others—but respond it did.

When American education was caught up in the "developmental values" craze, the publishers produced a flood of books that taught young children to pick up their toys or be kind to their pets.

Religion is an excellent example of an important and often controversial category about which we cannot today claim to have a library collection reflecting a wide range of viewpoints. In juvenile nonfiction, there are very few books about religion, and all represent traditional views of the subject. For instance, there is no *Child's Guide to Atheism* to balance *One God: The Ways We Worship Him.*

As members of a profession dedicated to providing free access to ideas for all people, librarians must take steps to help broaden the viewpoints available in children's materials. First, we can commit ourselves to buying children's books that contain attitudes not presently represented in the collection *regardless of the quality of writing.* In fact, our collection policy might well contain the statement: "Ordinary standards will be waived for materials representing a point of view not found in the collection." Only by purchasing first efforts, however inadequate, can we demonstrate to publishers the need for materials expressing a particular viewpoint.

Second, we can offer concrete support to reviewers who come under attack from the more conservative members of our profession. It is disheartening to see how few positive letters are written to the editors of *Booklist* or *School Library Journal* supporting their attempts to review a broader range of materials for libraries. For every "please-cancel-my-subscription"–type letter they receive now, the editors should receive a hundred telling them how appreciative librarians are of their efforts.

Finally, within our professional organizations at the local, state, regional, and national levels, we can demand programs that examine the narrowness of juvenile publishing, thereby alerting publishers that the profession as-a-whole is concerned with opening up the world of ideas for children. We should systematically analyze all of juvenile publishing to identify as many categories as possible that have similar limitations. The more knowledge we have, the better able we are to work toward helping eliminate the restrictions.

DEVELOPING A PHILOSOPHICAL POSITION

We need the type of knowledge discussed above, but we also need philosophical guidelines within which to function. Since poets say things better than other people, I would like to base this discussion on the following two poems:

LIES [2]
by Yevgeny Yevtushenko

Telling lies to the young is wrong.
Proving to them that lies are true is wrong.
Telling them that God's in his heaven
and all's well with the world is wrong.
The young know what you mean. The young are people.
Tell them the difficulties can't be counted,
and let them see not only what will be
but see with clarity these present times.
Say obstacles exist they must encounter
sorrow happens, hardship happens.
The hell with it. Who never knew
the price of happiness will not be happy.
Forgive no error you recognize,
it will repeat itself, increase,
and afterwards our pupils
will not forgive in us what we forgave.

TRUTH [3]
by May Sarton

Not visible
After all
Through a glass table,
Air, or crystal
Of open window,
Transparent door,
But less, or more—
A prism maybe,
Now blue, now green,
And what you see
I have not seen.
For change the eye
And what was true
Becomes a lie:
My green, your blue.
For who can tell

Just what was said?
None hears it all:
Your blue, my red.
The human truth
Is hard to sift,
Alack, forsooth,
Is apt to shift.
Facet by facet,
Never vicarious,
Definite, tacit,
The light is various.
My truth, your lie,
My lie, your truth.
See eye to eye?
Alack—forsooth—

Lies and *Truth* present an interesting dichotomy. Is it possible simultaneously to believe that telling lies to the young is wrong and to accept the fact that "my truth" may be "your lie"? Can we say in a collection policy that we will not buy materials that lie to children and also recognize that there are many different ways of viewing the truth? Looked at that way, the question of developing a library collection moves into the realm of philosophy and becomes a problem of ethics.

Although we find it possible to accept the general idea that each school of philosophy has its own view of truth, it may still be disconcerting to discover that the principles and values upon which we base our own practical decisions are not necessarily shared or even recognized by those around us. The problem is not an academic one. Librarians are called upon to apply their values to real-life situations. The personal views that may influence our decisions to accept or reject materials for our libraries may be in fundamental conflict with those of our colleagues or our patrons; and such conflict can have a strong, even unpleasant, effect on many people, including, of course, ourselves.

Now, a collection policy, while it is the most useful tool for identifying areas of conflict and for creating a community-wide awareness that different points of view can and ought to co-exist in the shelves of a library, cannot ward off all disputes over the nature of "appropriate" materials. We must go further than the community level. We must develop and articulate a strong philosophical position from which the library profession as a whole can operate. The present American Library Association position on intellectual freedom is based on law rather than on philosophy. Specifically it is based on the First Amendment to the Constitution of the United States which says: "Congress shall make no law abridging the freedom of speech, or of the press . . ."

There are a number of problems with the ALA's position, each of which would require an entire chapter to detail. The following brief discussion is designed to alert readers to the complexities of the issue and to provoke, one hopes, further reading and thinking on the subject.

First of all, no Supreme Court in the entire history of the United States has accepted the purist view of the First Amendment. An occasional Justice, such as Hugo Black, has himself been a purist, but the Court itself has never been willing to say that there are no limits on free speech. What this means is that the ALA position on intellectual freedom offers librarians a view of the First Amendment that may do them no good in a court of law.

It is difficult enough to keep up with what the Court does consider the limits on free speech without confusing the issue by acting as if there were no limits at all. In large measure, the First Amendment means whatever the present Court says it does and nothing more. Thus, the limits on free speech expand or contract according to the makeup of the Supreme Court.

A second, and from my point of view, larger problem with the ALA position is that it leaves no room for negotiation between librarians and their communities. By taking the purist view of the First Amendment, ALA encourages us to see all complaints about materials in our collections as representing threats to democracy and free speech. The domino theory, rejected by liberals in the field of foreign policy, is accepted enthusiastically by them when it comes to the removal of books from libraries.

11

Remove one book and soon all books will be gone, is the underlying message of the ALA position.

That stance represents total nonsense. Librarians can and do make mistakes as they add materials to the collection. Books do become outdated and should be systematically removed from the collection. There are reasons for weeding a collection other than physical deterioration. Judgment was used in adding the materials (one hopes), and judgment should be used in removing them.

Inherent in the ALA position is a basic contempt for the good sense of both librarians and the members of the communities we serve. ALA seems to feel that a rigid policy is the only way it can keep us in line, that left to our own discretion, we would impose our personal biases on the total collection, admitting no views with which we disagree. Now, it is true that some librarians exercise a great deal of censorship upon their collections. Marjorie Fiske proved that point in *Book Selection and Censorship*[4] (1959), and everything Fiske found in her sample of California school and public libraries will remain true for some libraries until doomsday. The facts, however, are that the last fifteen years have seen more librarians working to expand the range of materials within their collections than ever before.

A third problem with the ALA position is that it focuses almost exclusively on patron-inspired attacks to remove materials while it ignores librarian-inspired actions, like the refusal to purchase controversial materials. In my opinion, the failure to buy materials represents a far greater threat to free speech than the occasional removal of a title. The failure to buy materials penalizes the poor, the young, the aged—all those who have neither the money nor the access to the distribution channels that librarians have.

Finally, the fundamental flaw in assuming a purely legalistic position is that we ignore the question of whether free access to information is a basic human right (which is what philosophy is all about) or whether it is a matter of law (which is what jurisprudence is all about). If the latter is the case, then free access is dependent upon the legal provisions of a particular country. Not only do civil rights for citizens vary from country to country, but even within the United States there exists a wide range of state laws and local ordinances. If we can perceive any universal justification for people having the right of free access to information, then we should be able to develop an argument based as much upon principle as on legal tradition.

We must begin a philosophical discussion by asking whether free speech is an end or a means. The purist view assumes that free speech in and of itself is a "good." This position is similar to that taken by many scientists in the pre-atomic bomb days: pure research had led to the creation of the bomb and only afterwards did some scientists ask themselves if the ability to destroy the earth was a worthwhile achievement. If the analogy with atomic weaponry seems melodramatic, think about the number of phrases used by intellectual freedom defenders that equate "the pen" with "the sword."

I fully recognize the dangers in saying that for free speech to be "good" it must be directed toward the achievement of positive goals. All of us involved in the defense of intellectual freedom know how easy it is for "good" to mean simply what is politically expedient. For example, in *Ceremony of Innocence*, James Forman's novel about young people fighting Hitler inside Germany, one of the Nazi interrogators says, "But our National Socialist dream, if it is to become a reality, demands certain incidental inhumanities."[5] Besides the murder of Jews, Gypsies, homosexuals, and political deviants, those "incidental inhumanities" included the total suppression of free speech—all in the name of the greater good of the Third Reich. In the United States and Canada, we built no gas chambers. We simply "relocated" citizens of Japanese descent, taking from them their homes, their businesses, their jobs, destroying the fabric of their lives.

History is filled with similar examples, and I cite these two not just because they happened in my lifetime, but because they could happen only because of a basic racist attitude within the countries involved. That is why, in my opinion, all of us who care about intellectual freedom have to care equally about elim-

13

inating racism from our society, for racists in power act quickly to curtail the freedoms of all who disagree with them.

Taking a purist view of freedom of speech is more comfortable than dealing with the constant decisions necessitated by a more flexible view. Walter Kaufmann, one of America's most important philosophers, has coined the word *decidophobia* in connection with purists, who prefer to make one decision in order to avoid having to make any other decisions. [6]

But professionals are paid to make decisions and our communities expect professionally educated librarians to exercise judgment. Most members of our communities do not want a library collection devoid of controversial materials, but they do want some lines drawn. This is particularly true when it comes to children's access to materials. The children's librarian could not, for example, defend the library's purchase of hard-core pornographic magazines for the children's collection and expect community support for such a position.

Interpersonal Relations

To ignore the limitations most people want imposed in certain areas of free expression is to ignore a basic psychological need. Intellectual freedom purists assume that logic is the ultimate weapon in human affairs, but in fact it plays a very small role in how well we function in our professional and personal lives. The myth that proclaims logic superior to emotion is as destructive as the idea that feeling is automatically superior to intellect. Fortunately for the human race, most of us who function in the real world (as opposed to psychotic worlds) cannot be totally logical or totally emotional.

I have asked dozens of librarians, "How do you feel when someone complains about the library owning a particular book or magazine?" The answer, whether it comes immediately or after considerable discussion, is almost invariably, "Defensive."

That is a normal response. When we work hard to do a good job, when we care about what we are doing, criticism can make us feel inadequate. How we handle this feeling can often be the difference between defusing and provoking a potentially explosive situation.

If we understand that someone must feel threatened by a book to complain about it, we can usually defuse the situation by employing the art of active listening as described by Thomas Gordon in *P.E.T.* (Parent Effectiveness Training).[7] Saying something as simple as "I can see this book upset you" can turn the subsequent exchange into a discussion rather than a battle. It is important to recognize and accept the person's feelings before going into a discussion of substantive issues. This caring about how people feel permeates the rest of this book in one way or another. Some people seem to have these interpersonal skills as part of their personality; most of us have to work very hard at acquiring them. We may decide to begin learning these skills for strictly pragmatic reasons—to learn how to handle complaints without making the people angrier than they were when they arrived. But eventually, we discover that we like ourselves better for caring more about how people feel than about how they think.

There is no sense in learning the skills needed to build a good library collection if our lack of interpersonal skills negates our efforts. These skills will help us in all aspects of our professional —and personal—lives: we will be better able to defend what we do without becoming defensive; we will have better relationships with staff members, and we will treat the children who come to our libraries with more respect.

NOTES FOR CHAPTER 1

1. Duane H. Meyers, "Boys and Girls and Sex and Libraries," *Library Journal*, February 15, 1977, pp. 457–463; See also editorial in same issue for excellent statement of the power of community support.
2. Yevgeny Yevtushenko, *Yevtushenko: Selected Poems*, Baltimore: Pergamon, 1963.
3. May Sarton, *Land of Silence and Other Poems*, New York: Rinehart, 1953, p. 50.
4. Marjorie Fiske, *Book Selection and Censorship; A Study of School and Public Libraries in California*, Berkeley: University of California Press, 1959.
5. James Forman, *Ceremony of Innocence*, New York: Dell, 1977, p. 17.
6. Walter Kaufmann, *Without Guilt or Justice; From Decidophobia to Autonomy*, New York: Delta, 1975, pp. 1–34.
7. Thomas Gordon, *P.E.T. Parent Effectiveness Training*, New York: New Am. Lib. 1975.

CHAPTER TWO

Selection Standards

THE MOMENT the word *standard* is introduced we must keep firmly in mind that it presupposes a norm against which something can be measured. In our case, that something is usually a book. The book can meet the standard, fall below it, or rise above it.

Unlike many other standards that can be set with a reasonable degree of objectivity, library standards are bound to be subjectively established and subjectively applied. Deciding what are the ingredients of "a good book" is very different from determining how many units of vitamin D should be in every quart of milk sold.

There are many books (listed in Chapter 10 and in the bibliography under "Selection Tools") that discuss the traditional criteria for selection used by librarians. This chapter takes a nontraditional approach to the subject in the hope that once certain confusions are identified, the traditional criteria will assume a new meaning.

SUBJECTIVITY

There are people who think that it is unprofessional for librarians to let their personal values show on the job. These people subscribe to the myth of objectivity. They seem to believe that as we enter a library or school, we not only can, but should, leave our personal selves and experiences behind.

17

I will explain why I do not count myself among the believers in objectivity. There are now available to us hundreds of psychological studies that show that our personal biases (almost always buried in the unconscious) keep us from being objective. In one study, for example, two identical job résumés were prepared, one carrying a male name, the other a female name. Those ranking the résumés rated the male better qualified every time. In college psychology classrooms, students have witnessed scenes of violence performed by two actors, a black and a white. Even when the black was the victim, many of the students perceived him as the attacker. In these studies, and hundreds of others, the participants claimed to believe in equality. They were not in any way conscious sexists or racists.[1]

It is, of course, possible to acquire a level of consciousness that minimizes the influence that our conditioned biases can exercise on our decisions. Such a level of awareness requires (1) recognition that we have a certain biased perception; (2) willingness to change; and (3) countless hours of reading and research that will provide us with new insights.

None of us has the time or inclination to change all of our conditioned responses, so at best, as mature adults, we may manage to achieve a level of objectivity in two or three areas we consider important. We should bear in mind that this process is an exchange of unconsciously-held values for consciously-held values. It is not a process that makes us *valueless*. It defines and enhances our values by making them articulate, part of our conscious self over which we have control.

I believe that we have a responsibility to share our values with the people we work with and for. When I was a professor in a library school, I used to tell my students precisely where I stood on whatever issue was under discussion. Not only did this give them something concrete to respond to, but it also forced them to define their own beliefs. In the ensuing discussions, all parties learned a very important lesson: we learned that we could disagree without disliking one another. Sometimes, their arguments changed my thinking; sometimes it was the students who did the changing; often, of course, none of us changed, but we were all made increasingly aware that people we like and respect can hold different opinions and operate under different values. Students who learn that lesson in library school have learned what intellectual freedom is all about.

Most librarians in schools and public libraries are reluctant to articulate their value system. Some are afraid of trouble in their communities. These are the librarians who are surprised when they find the censor has knocked at their door.

There is a basic dishonesty in concealing from others the principles under which we operate. There may also be a basic contempt for other people. We may be saying, "You are too dumb (too narrow-minded, too something) to be treated as an equal." Unconsciously, of course, we may be so unsure of our own values that we do not dare expose them in the marketplace.

Discovering Values

The following hypothetical examples are just a few of many that can help us determine the limits of our value systems.

If someone were to publish a book for elementary school–age children that maintained that smoking, drinking, and drug use were good methods of increasing one's enjoyment in life, would you buy the book? Would it make a difference if you were the librarian in an elementary school with a good drug-education program?

If someone were to publish a book for children that told them that if they were having trouble with someone, it would be perfectly all right, when all else failed, to punch that person in the nose or otherwise physically assault him or her, would you buy the book?

If someone were to publish a book that supported Arthur Jensen's theory[2] that blacks have a lower IQ than other people, would you buy it? Would it make a difference to you if the book's point was that a technological society cannot afford people with low IQs and that such people should be sterilized; or, if the book's point was that all people are entitled to life with respect and dignity regardless of their intelligence as measured by the majority society?

If someone wrote a book for children that told them that it cost society too much money to support mentally and physically disabled people and such people should be put to death, would you buy it?

19

The one thing these four examples have in common is their focus on the attitudes expressed toward the topics and not on the accuracy or inaccuracy of the information being conveyed. Whether you have answered the questions *yes, no,* or *maybe,* does not matter. If you will examine the values you hold that led you to your answers, you will be one step further along the road to consciously defining the value structure under which you operate. The next step is to find a small group of people, including some you do not particularly relate to, with whom you can discuss these and other examples of value-laden questions. Self-analysis can carry us just so far; then we must be able to discuss with others how we feel and, if necessary, to develop the rationale that enables us to defend our positions.

TRADITIONAL ASSUMPTIONS AND RESULTING CONFUSIONS

The selection of materials for children is potentially one of the most explosive issues in librarianship today. Besides our failure to articulate the value structure under which we operate, there are three other factors that have gotten us into our present trouble: (1) our criteria have been too vague; (2) we have imposed adult values upon children; and (3) we have acted as if one standard, or one set of standards, was applicable to all types of books.

Vagueness

We have been fond of asking such questions as "Is the character believable?" It is a vague and useless question unless we go on to ask, "Believable to whom?" Librarians of my generation remember well the controversy that flared with the publication of Louise Fitzhugh's *Harriet the Spy* (1964). The pages of *School Library Journal*[3] for late 1964 and early 1965 were filled with views on the book and even the *Horn Book* editor entered the fray.[4] The issue, seen in retrospect, was not whether Harriet was believable, but whether she was likable, which is a very different question. One of the unspoken criteria for children's books, then and now, is that unlikable characters must be punished.

We see this principle operating in many stories. If an author

20

depicts a bigot, the bigot must be shown as a social deviate. The bigots in children's books are never allowed to have the majority on their side or to triumph. In sports books, athletes who break training or who cheat are always caught. They never walk off with Olympic gold medals. Unlikable characters can escape punishment only by reforming or repenting. Such behavior does not make the characters believable, but it does satisfy the unarticulated but ever-present value system most of us bring to children's book evaluation.

Another vague question we like to ask is: "Is this story true to life?" For example, Bette Greene's *Summer of My German Soldier* and Marjorie Kellogg's *Like the Lion's Tooth* are two very powerful books about children who are physically abused by their parents as well as emotionally deprived. There are people, and some of them are librarians, who do not believe these books are true to life. Again, the question must be expanded to ask, "True to whose life?" When books treat major social problems, the reluctance to ask the latter part of the question is understandable since if we admit the reality of the world the books depict, then we as adults must also assume some responsibility for allowing that world to exist. If our personal value system does not allow us to accept such social responsibility, we will find all kinds of reasons for rejecting books that would force that responsibility upon us.

It is essential that we clarify for ourselves, if for no one else, what each of us means when we talk about believable characters and plots that are true to life. A technique that I have found that works for me (courtesy of Robert Samples' and Robert Wohlford's book *Opening*[5]) is to stop asking *why* questions and focus on *what* questions. I no longer ask myself, "*Why* do I like or not like this book?" Instead, I ask, "*What* does this book make me feel?"

If a book makes me feel threatened, angry, depressed, or guilty, it stands to reason that I am not going to "like" it. Recognizing this, I am sometimes able to accept it by saying, "Well, it's not my kind of book, but I can see its appeal to others." Sometimes I have to remove myself from making a judgment about it at all and accept someone else's evaluation. If a book I

21

dislike receives favorable reviews in all the major reviewing periodicals, I have to accept the fact that it is I who am out of step and not the rest of the profession. This process of learning to trust other people's judgments is as important as learning to trust one's own.

There is a not-so-negligible fringe benefit to this approach. It helps us deal fairly with people whose views differ from our own, even with adults who want books removed from the library's shelves. If I learn to accept the validity of my own feelings (and it is not essential to take the next step and analyze *why* I am experiencing those feelings) it is easier to accept other people's feelings. If, instead of thinking of people who complain about books as, say, neo-fascists, we think of them as people whose value systems have been shaken by the book they are attacking, I am convinced that we would be able to have more discussions and fewer confrontations with them. If we were to begin every such discussion by saying, "I can see that this book upset you," instead of asking either in words or body language, "Why are you upset?" we would all be better off. Every time we ask "why" we are demanding that other people justify their feelings, which only infuriates them.

Robert Samples, who specializes in helping people achieve self-actualization, has written:

> In working in my intimate laboratory, as well as with others, the most shocking thing I have come to realize about myself is that I cannot remember ever having made a rational decision about a significant problem. In every instance of significant decision making that I am able to trace to a source, the decision has been made on an emotional-intuitive premise. Later, of course, when explaining the reasons for my decision to other people, I became incredibly rational and objective, weaving a great tapestry of logic to hang about the edges of my emotional-intuitive decision.
>
> I tested this insight with groups of teachers and students in over a dozen large city school districts. The results corroborated my belief. Nearly every decision a person makes is based on emotion and intuition, not logic and rationality. [6]

As librarians concerned with interpersonal communication, we would do well to pay attention to Samples' insights.

Imposing Adult Standards

We impose adult standards on children, but none so consistently as adult *literary* standards. We should certainly assume responsibility for building a library collection that offers children access to the best writing, past and present. But I also believe that we should offer children access to materials that children want—comic books and popular series titles. This is a view I have come to adopt in recent years, and it is a change of opinion that requires explanation.

I began my professional career surrounded by selection dicta. One did not buy Nancy Drew, the Bobbsey Twins, the Hardy Boys, or Tom Swift. (Depending on the library system one worked for, one did not buy *Stuart Little, The Wizard of Oz,* or *Pippi Longstocking* either, but that is another story.) Some librarians did stock the series books, of course, but they did not admit to this practice in the presence of other professionals.

I must confess that a book like *Tom Swift Jr. & the Cosmic Astronauts* assaults every nerve in my body. I am annoyed not only by a writing style that labels every character ("Tom, the young inventor"; "Felix Wong, the Chinese-American") but also by the silliness of the plot. When the time that elapses between Tom's idea for a new aircraft and its test flight is only a matter of days, my sense of reality is offended. It is, quite literally, painful for me to read one of the series books.

It has taken me most of my adult life to understand that the very characteristics of series books that offend me most are what make the books so appealing to young readers. As long as I read only library literature and remained ignorant of important research into children's psychological, intellectual, and moral development, I could feel virtuous while using sentimental (actually, wishful) views of childhood to support my decisions in book selection.

Young readers of series books—usually elementary school students—are not at a stage in either their moral or intellectual development to cope with fine distinctions or shades of gray in the delineation of character. The fact that in the series books the reader can know from the moment a character is introduced whether she or he is a good or bad person is important to children. Children's sense of time is such that it seems natural to them for events to move rapidly. They do not worry about the facts of a technological society—the years between the time an idea is conceived and the time it is first tested. If we really mean it when we say that a book should be appropriate for its potential readers, then the series books must be judged among the most appropriate of all children's books.

A second way in which we impose adult standards is by taking for granted the ability to read fluently and rapidly. Where children's books are concerned, we tend to read the entire volume, or a large chunk of it, in one sitting; children often read one chapter at a time. The constant repetition in the series books bores us, but it serves to remind children "who is who" when they pick up the book the next day or a week later.

If we are confirmed adult readers—and it is important to remember that not all librarians are readers—we may tend to forget that before there can be literary enjoyment, there must first be reading skills. Like all other skills, reading requires practice and in the beginning it does not matter whether that practice is a series book or the cereal box on the breakfast table.

Finally, I want to talk about the damage we do to children's self-esteem when we stand in our libraries and say, contemptuously, "We wouldn't have *those* books in the library!" We will never know how many children have grown to adulthood believing the library exists only for some mythical elite to which they can never belong. Certainly, the low percentage of adult readers on the North American continent suggests that schools and libraries are not doing as much as they ought for young readers.

In no other area of knowledge do we hold children responsible for meeting adult standards. Why should we expect them to share our tastes in literature? I have come to believe that the only way to acquire genuine literary taste—one's own and not externally imposed—is through wide and continuous reading. If providing titles from each popular series will give us the opportunity to suggest other books to the devoted readers of Tom

Swift or Nancy Drew, then I believe that the opportunity outweighs any conceivable harm that might be done to so-called literary standards.

Just as I believe we must learn not to ask people to justify their feelings, so have I come to believe that people—a word that includes children—have a right to like books without our approval. This does not mean that we should not do everything possible to create a rapport with children so that we can offer guidance in a friendly, open way. When the time is right, we can say, "I don't know how you stand reading those books. They drive me crazy." If we have become a trusted friend, the child may respond, "Why?" and we can explain, as long as we stick to the facts and are not carried away with making judgments. An example of a factual, nonjudgmental statement is, "It drives me crazy to know that Nancy Drew is always going to solve the case, and I even know how she'll do it by chapter three." This sort of explanation conveys to the child feelings and opinions without requiring that the child feel or think the same way. Some children, maybe most, will respond with, "But that's why I like the books," and we will have learned something. A few children may ponder our words and say then or later, "Yeah, you're right. Maybe that's why they're beginning to bore me."

Only when the children, not we, have had enough are they ready to move on. Our job is not to push children into motion, but to be there to point out a new road when they are ready for one.

Single vs. Multiple Standards

Many of us operate on the assumption that a single standard or set of standards can be applied to all types of books. But some types of books such as those on sex education (see Chapter 4) must be judged by more complicated criteria than others. In this section, I want to explore the problem of dirty words in children's books and conclude by raising a few questions about other types of books that may lead readers to ask their own questions. We can begin with one of the vague questions we have pretended was a helpful standard: "Is the language appropriate for the age level for which the book is intended?" When this question was first asked in years past, it usually had to do with the sophistication of the language and it evoked arguments over vocabulary control and other pedagogic responses. Today, it often means that we are talking about words our culture labels obscene or blasphemous.

To put the problem into perspective we have to take a short trip back in history to 1961, when I reviewed Frick's *Comeback Guy* for *School Library Journal.*[7] A subsequent letter to the editor raised the question of whether reviewers have an obligation to alert librarians when a book contains profanity. I did not remember any profanity in *Comeback Guy*, so I reread it and still did not find any. I gave it to a colleague and she did not find any. Finally, a third reader said hesitantly, "Do you suppose it's the quote from the Steig cartoon?"

One of the most famous of William Steig's cartoons (still found on cocktail napkins) shows an oddball sitting in a box, his hands on top of his head, his head bent in dejection. The caption reads, "People are no damn good." It was such an appropriate rendering of how the book's central character felt that it seemed impossible anyone would object to its use.

As the three of us talked about the situation, we began to ask ourselves whether the charge of profanity was not merely the *excuse* for objecting to the book and whether the real *reason* did not lie elsewhere. Since the letter writer came from what is loosely called "the Bible Belt," we felt it was possible that the real crime in the book was that the hero loaded kegs of beer onto trucks. True, he did not drink the beer—did not, in fact, even see it—but clearly the author did not object to the existence of beer. We may, of course, have reached a wrong conclusion, but since nothing in the book seemed to warrant the charge of profanity, we could only hypothesize.

That all took place in 1961–62, and I would have considered it ancient history except that the October 1974 issue of *Wilson Library Bulletin* contained a piece, "Take Cuss Words Out of Kids' Books,"[8] which said my review of *Comeback Guy* represented some kind of turning of the scales in favor of letting obscenities creep into children's books. That is distorting history (reread *Johnny Tremain*, for example, which was published in

1943), but since it is true that there are more cuss words in children's books these days, the matter deserves further discussion.

If I were reviewing a cookbook for children and the recipe read, "Take the damn flour and add it to the sugar and butter," I would find that offensive and inappropriate. People who manifest aggression against inanimate objects like flour frighten me. It is the implication of the sentence that would bother me, not the word damn *per se.*

If I were reviewing an easy-to-read book for second graders and the author wrote, "Janie was angry because her fucking bicycle would not go up the hill," I would object. Besides, again, using the obscenity in relationship to an inanimate object, the sentence would be offensive because in this context it seems clearly to be a gratuitous statement by the author and not what the character could be expected to utter. In children's books, as indeed in adult books, the use of obscenities must be considered appropriate or inappropriate in relation to the characters and their situation. Otherwise, bad language is simply bad writing, and no moral judgment need be made in order to reject the book. Librarians operating under the standard that language must be appropriate to the character would have no trouble accepting John Steptoe's *My Special Best Words,* [9] where the words stink and pee, both of which are in wide usage among preschoolers, are mentioned.

If there are some librarians who are upset by an occasional hell or damn in a book, there are many more who find it difficult to accept the four-letter words shit and fuck. What circumstances make either or both of these words appropriate?

John Neufeld attacked this problem in *Freddy's Book,* [10] which is pretty poor fiction but an instructive book for adults because of the way in which the author deals with four-letter words. Freddy has discovered the word fuck and is on a search to discover its meaning. His mother tries hard to explain it to him, but she is so vague that he is left more confused than he was when he began. Being a good library user, Freddy goes to the library for enlightenment. Every librarian who is uncomfortable with spoken obscenities should read the scene that occurs in the library.

27

A friend of mine who is a public health specialist uses *Freddy's Book* in her course at a school of nursing to point out to students that they have to be free enough to deal with patients on the patients' terms. If people cannot talk to us in their vocabulary without our making moral judgments, we have closed off the communication channels. Neither public health nurses nor librarians have to make such words as fuck part of their own everyday language, but it is very important that we learn not to be shocked or dismayed at their use by others. The point in developing and articulating one's own value system is to understand that it *is* one's own and that it is not to be imposed upon others. This is not an easy concept for many white, middle-class North Americans, who have been raised to believe that their standards are the norm against which all others are to be measured. It is particularly difficult for people over forty who grew up in an era when cursing as a form of speech was seen as part of the lower class's uncouth behavior patterns. Much of that has changed today. The use of obscenities is a part of many people's lives—taken for granted—and is no longer viewed as a matter of social class.

Even if children do not hear obscenities at home, it is unlikely that they will not hear the words from their peers or encounter them on a wall in this graffiti-covered world. We want children to grow up having as much intellectual curiosity as possible, and this means we must be willing to help them learn whatever it is they want to know at the time they want to know it. If a child wants to know the meaning of fuck and we indicate by our facial expressions and words that it is an unacceptable question, then the next time the child wants to know something, she or he may be very hesitant about asking. We will have conveyed the message that there are areas of knowledge of which we disapprove. Since children have no way of anticipating what other areas of questions may evoke our disapproval, most of them will soon stop asking and we will have contributed to a stifling of their intellect. That is a very high price to ask people to pay for enforcing what is, after all, only a matter of personal taste.

Before leaving this subject, there is another point I would like to make about imposing one's religious beliefs onto the library's collection. I distinguish between religion and morality and do not see the terms as synonymous. In the article "Take Cuss Words Out of Kids' Books," the author also considers such expressions as My God! to be in the same category as four-letter words. She describes herself as "subscribing to the Judaic-Christian teaching opposed to the taking of the name of God in vain." [11] However much our religion means to us, we should be aware of the dangers inherent in imposing it as a standard upon a library collection. We may feel that our religion represents God's will—in fact, it wouldn't be a religious belief if that were not the case—but we must also consider what would happen to library collections if librarians who were Christian Scientists refused to buy books about the medical and health professions, or if vegetarian librarians refused to buy books in which people ate meat or cookbooks in which meat dishes appeared. If we do not want a small vocal group of citizens in our communities imposing their values on the library's collection, we must be sure that we are not imposing our own. Having said that, I reiterate that this does not mean there will not be times when we can properly object to obscenities in children's books and do so without feeling guilty.

BOOKS FROM OTHER COUNTRIES

Anne Pellowski, one of the world's authorities on internationalism in children's books, has asked the following question in relationship to evaluating folkloric and fictional materials:

> Has it been edited to remove all elements which are morally or socially not accepted in our culture, or have some of these intrinsic values of the society concerned been allowed to remain intact, e.g., polygamy, matter-of-fact acceptance of body functions, early marriage or love relationships? [12]

When Americans have written children's books about other lands they have tended to treat the mores of those countries as quaint rather than as integral parts of a real culture. As Third World countries develop economically however, they will be creating their own publishing industries and eventually they will produce books that will become part of the world's juvenile literature. It is not too early, then, to begin thinking about how we will handle the cultural differences.

The improved relationship with China, for instance, may see more Chinese children's books available, which will raise the question of whether the literature is political propaganda. When children's books present American political propaganda, which most of our history and historical fiction books do, we tend to view that as "accurate." Every country tends to use children's literature as a vehicle for transmitting the views the "establishment" wants children to have. In an article titled, "A Sword With Two Edges: The Role of Children's Literature in the Writings of N. K. Krupskaia," Boris Raymond describes Krupskaia's views:

> A typical product of the nineteenth-century Russian populist intelligentsia, she was deeply distrustful of tradition and of religion and, conversely, had an almost unbounded faith in the efficacy of reason and of science as alternate guides for human betterment. The book, for her, was an enormously powerful but dangerous weapon. Although she never indulged in the kind of oversimplifications which are associated with the name of Zhdanov, there is in her writing an element of absolutism, expecially when she discusses the kinds of books that should be made available to children and to the "unprepared reader." For her there were positive books—the ones which led their readers toward a greater scientific understanding, books that elevated and uplifted—and then there were books which had a negative influence. She believed that through a proper understanding of Marxism-Leninism it was possible to distinguish between the two kinds, and that the circulation of good books needed to be promoted, whereas bad books should not be made available. Coming during the formative period of Soviet children's literature, Krupskaia's views helped shape the basic guidelines which, even today, determine Russian literary practice. [13]

By changing a few words in the above paragraph, we have a statement of the purposes of children's literature in all countries. For instance, American authors have been reluctant to treat the question of polygamy even in the historical context of Mormonism, a condition that should alert us to the depth of the problem. In a more specific example, the much-praised *A Day No Pigs Would Die*[14] by Robert Newton Peck purports to be a story of Shaker life. Yet Peck has his adult characters married and parents—both states contrary to Shaker principles, which is one reason why the sect has not grown. It is difficult to understand why an author would make a subject like the Shaker religion an intrinsic part of a book and then distort its presentation. If we cannot depict honestly the divergent values within our own culture, it is doubtful that we will be receptive to values from totally different cultures. Yet learning that *different* does not mean *inferior* is vital if we are going to live together in reasonable harmony.

NONFICTION CONCERNS

This is a true story: In the small Connecticut town where I grew up, the Unitarian minister was judged too old for his position, so the congregation retired him as "minister emeritus" and the Library Board of Trustees appointed him head librarian. Eventually, he was made "librarian emeritus" and it was then discovered that he had classified all books on religion according to his personal beliefs. Those books he approved of were placed in the Dewey 200s; those that met with his disapproval went into the 398s as folklore!

The way we classify materials and the subject headings we assign to them constitute value judgments. We bring those same value judgments to the selection process and we need to be aware that we are doing so.

Traditionally we approach nonfiction by asking whether the information is accurate. This is a valid question for all nonfiction materials. For some books it is the only question. We can evaluate a cookbook by randomly sampling the recipes and if the specified ingredients produce the promised product, we know the book has validity. We can follow the instructions in a how-to-do-it book and see whether we can make the object the author promises us.

But if the how-to-do-it book contains instructions on how to make a bomb—and they work—suddenly the accuracy of information becomes a danger. While it is unlikely that a children's book would offer such instructions, the example serves to highlight the role that value judgments play in the selection process. We want accurate information, but we also want it to serve positive purposes.

"To serve positive purposes" is one of those vague phrases that we can all concur in until we try to analyze exactly what we mean by "positive." Few of us would feel that teaching children to make bombs constituted a positive purpose. Many citizens of the United States would feel that a book that presented life in Communist China as "better" than life under Chiang Kai-shek was not serving a positive purpose, because to these citizens the form of government, rather than the quality of the average person's existence, is what makes life "better" or "worse" in a particular country. Yet other citizens would feel that it serves no positive purpose to have American children grow up thinking that democracy is the only form of government under which people can live happy, productive lives. The contradictions do not end there. Some of the people who would accept a book that showed people happy under a communist government would object to one that showed people living happy, ordinary lives under a fascist dictatorship.

SUMMARY

If we ask the wrong questions, or if we ask the right questions without examining our underlying assumptions, we are almost certain to find that our selection standards are dominated by our personal value system. It is natural to believe that our value system is valid, acceptable, and worthwhile—otherwise we would not hold to it. What takes both professional and personal maturity is the recognition that our value system is ours and is not to be imposed, directly or subtly, upon others. When more librarians understand this, we may be able to devise ways to convey the message to members of our communities as well.

NOTES FOR CHAPTER 2

1. For studies in racism/sexism perceptions, see the bibliography under the heading "Racism and Sexism."
2. Arthur R. Jensen, "How Much Can We Boost I.Q. and Scholastic Achievement?" *Harvard Educational Review*, Winter, 1969, pp. 1–123.
3. For the *Harriet the Spy* controversy, *see* Dorothy M. Broderick, "The Spy Who Got Locked in the Ice Box," *School Library Journal*, March 1965, pp. 114–15; Letter to the Editor, *School Library Journal*, February 1965, p. 4.
4. Ruth Hill Viguers, "Of Spies and Applesauce and Such," *Horn Book*, February 1965, pp. 74–6.
5. Robert Samples, and Robert Wohlford, *Opening*. Reading, MA: Addison-Wesley, 1975.
6. Robert Samples, "Value Prejudice: Toward a Personal Awareness," *Media & Methods*, September 1974, pp. 49+.
7. The original review of Frick's *Comeback Guy* appeared in *School Library Journal*, April 1961, p. 58. For the subsequent controversy, *see* Letters to the Editor, *School Library Journal*, April, May, September, November 1962.
8. Eva Nelson, "Take Cuss Words Out of Kids' Books," *Wilson Library Bulletin*, October 1974, pp. 132–3.
9. John Steptoe, *My Special Best Words*, New York: Viking, 1975.
10. John Neufeld, *Freddy's Book*, New York: Camelot Books (Avon), 1975, pp. 55–9.
11. Nelson, *op. cit.*
12. Anne Pellowski, "Internationalism in Children's Books," *in* Zena Sutherland and May Hill Arbuthnot, *Children and Books*, 5th ed., Glenview, IL: Scott, 1977, 615–19.
13. Boris Raymond, "A Sword With Two Edges: The Role of Children's Literature in the Writings of N. K. Krupskaia," *Library Quarterly*, vol. 44, no. 3, pp. 206–18.
14. Robert Newton Peck, *A Day No Pigs Would Die*, New York: Knopf, 1972.

The Ism Controversy

No PROBLEM within the library profession is more complex or more potentially explosive than the conflict between the principles of intellectual freedom and the commitment to eliminate racism, sexism, materialism, and other isms from children's materials. For two groups the solution is simple: the Council on Interracial Books for Children would have all books adhere to the line set down by the Council; the ALA Office for Intellectual Freedom, at the other end of the spectrum, believes that all attitudes should be allowed, however distasteful they may be to some.

Most of us fall somewhere in between these extreme positions. On the one hand, we understand that it takes time for children to develop the critical skills that allow them to evaluate diverse points of view—and that every major theory about human development tells us that not until the mid-teen years can human beings move outside themselves enough to be concerned with other people. On the other hand, we understand that the more social conditioning of whatever sort people receive, the harder it is for them to change, and we would not like children to be brain-washed by prevailing societal attitudes. Yet we also know that every book, well written or badly written, contains both the stated and the unstated views of the author. Authors live in society, have been conditioned by society, and are influenced by both current and traditional attitudes.

34

Before looking at the problems that confront us as librarians, I would like to talk about the rights of authors, the forgotten people in most discussions.

THE RIGHTS OF AUTHORS

Theoretically, authors have the right to decide the subject they will write about, the approach they will take to the subject, and the attitudes they will display toward the subject. That is theory. In practical terms, the narrow range of attitudes acceptable in children's books to the publishing community, which takes its cues from librarians, is a built-in restriction upon authors.

Authors who hope to be published today cannot write as outright racists. They cannot, for instance, depict Native Americans as savages. We can, of course, view this as a violation of the intellectual freedom of the author. Some of us, however, prefer to view it as a demand placed upon authors to depict people accurately, not as social mythology dictates. Whatever our view, we should be aware of the fact that we are placing restrictions upon the authors.

A concrete example of this point is Richard Peck's *Are You in the House Alone?* (1976),[1] which is about the rape of a high school student by her best friend's boyfriend. Five years ago the book probably would not have been published because there was little public discussion about rape, and taboo topics do not often find their way into books for children and teenagers.

It may seem mundane to observe that Peck in no way blames the victim, but had the book been written five or ten years ago, the chances are that the female would have been depicted as contributing to the rape, if not actually "asking for it." Today, well-informed people reject the "blaming the victim" syndrome; and just as it would have been difficult, if not impossible, to have a book on the subject of rape published five years ago, so is it difficult even to imagine a book for teenagers being published today that reflected the old attitude. (Adult books are an entirely different area and the above discussion does not apply to them.)

The constraints upon authors are many, and librarians would do well to keep that fact in mind. It is also important to keep in mind that what freedom for writers does exist within juvenile publishing is due to the courage of individual children's book editors and not to any action by children's librarians, who have not collectively demanded a wider range of materials for youthful readers.

The second point I want to make is that within the constraints imposed, an author has the right to limit the focus of his or her book to make the point he or she wants to make. A book that sets out to do one thing and do it well is more likely to be a good book than one in which the author wants to solve all the problems of the human race in less than two hundred pages. Again, the statement strikes me as painfully obvious, but it needs saying today more than ever. In an anonymously written article, "Old Values Surface in Blume Country,"[2] the author attacks Judy Blume for, among other things, setting her books in suburbia, having her characters be middle-class, being confused about racism, and portraying girls in traditional sex roles.

Content analysis of an author's collective writings is a bona-fide research method, but as librarians we must be sure that we understand the difference between good research techniques and poor ones. Content analyses are meant to describe accurately the content of books within context; they are meant to establish the author's purpose in writing the book, and make value judgments only in relationship to the author's purpose. *A content analysis should never attack an author for not doing something the author did not set out to do.*

Specifically, in the article on Judy Blume the writer attacks Blume because her "girl characters are into such things as shaving their legs and cosmetics *(It's Not the End of the World)* or are obsessed with bras and developing breasts like those of *Playboy* bunnies *(Are You There God? It's Me, Margaret)."* When we encounter such statements, we must learn to ask ourselves to take the time to analyze the unstated assumptions built into them. Are only hairy-legged females true feminists? If sexism is eliminated from society will girls—and boys, for that matter—cease to be excited, awed, and intrigued by the physical changes taking place during the maturation process?

Only as we learn to ask such questions and to recognize the

implications of the answers can we fulfill our obligation to preserve the author's right to write.

RACISM AND SEXISM IN LIBRARYLAND

Racism and sexism are often discussed together because none of us has a choice as to which racial group or which sex we will be born into. As Donnarae MacCann observed in her article "Children's Books in a Pluralistic Society":

> In this century special interest groups have been concerned about violent comic books, "subversive" history books, and increasingly explicit books about sex and/or sex education. These topics do not have the same bearing upon the child's emerging self-concept as do racism and sexism. The latter deal with qualities in a child that are invariable, and this fact places a different kind of responsibility upon those working with children.
>
> Questions of morality and patriotism call for discussion and the presentation of diverse viewpoints. There are many opinions to weigh and perspectives to balance. Children as well as adults have the right to encounter the various presentations. But a child's self-image in terms of race or sex is not a matter of degree. It is a necessary part of a child's being, and future development largely hinges upon it. In the long run society's future hinges upon it also, and the community therefore has the right to concern itself with children's self-concepts. [3]

The question facing children's librarians is simply stated: Do we, in the name of intellectual freedom, contribute to making nonwhite and female children feel like second-rate human beings because they were not born white males? The answer is more complicated than a resounding "no," and to understand why we must look at some events inside and outside the library profession that have occurred in the last decade.

The Developing Concern for the Rights of Youth

Until June 1967, the Library Bill of Rights did not contain the

37

word *age* in Article 5. Following a very successful preconference sponsored by ALA's Young Adult Services Division (YASD) and the ALA Intellectual Freedom Committee (IFC), the latter presented to Council an amendment to the Library Bill of Rights that made Article 5 read: "The rights of an individual to the use of a library should not be denied or abridged because of his age, race, religion, national origins or social or political views."

Having attended the 1967 ALA conference, I think it is fair to say that most of us in children's librarianship did not see the revised Library Bill of Rights as having anything to do with us. After all, the entire history of library work with children has centered around the concept that librarians are adult guides whose mission is to introduce children to the social values of adult society.

But in the late 1960s powerful forces were at work in society at large that cast doubt on the validity of this concept. Students began to challenge the school's right to dictate such matters as length of hair and style of dress; others, involved in the Vietnam peace movement, challenged the school's right to tell them they could not wear black armbands to protest the war.

In a series of important legal decisions in the late 1960s and 1970s, the United States Supreme Court and numerous lower courts established the principle that schools could not impose restrictions upon youth in matters that did not directly affect the educational process. In other words, school systems had no right to forbid girls to wear mini-skirts because such apparel *might* distract boys from their studies. [4]

In 1976 the Sixth Circuit U.S. Court of Appeals, in the case of *Susan Lee Minarcini, et al., v. Strongsville City School District*, took a large step forward in defending the rights of students to free access to information. The court ordered the school board to replace the books that it had voted to remove from the school library "by purchase, if necessary, out of the first sums available for library purposes." In reaching this decision, the court observed, "Here we are concerned with the right of students to receive information which they and their teachers desire them to have." The court also said that once a library is created, its use may not be restricted by "the social or political tastes of school board members." That statement is footnoted with one of the strongest defenses librarians anywhere could hope to receive from a legal ruling:

On the other hand, it would be consistent with the First Amendment (although not required by it) for every library in America to contain enough books so that every citizen in the community could find at least some which he or she regarded as objectionable in either subject matter, expression or idea.[5]

While this is a ruling of the Appeals Court, not the United States Supreme Court, and while it is binding only on the Strongsville City School Board, it has provided librarians with a potentially formidable precedent in defending library materials. It comes the closest to providing a legal basis for the Library Bill of Rights.

We must keep in mind that the courts, at all levels, do draw a distinction between library materials for borrowing and materials for sale. The U.S. Supreme Court ruled in *Ginzberg* v. *N.Y.* that the state was within its rights to forbid the sale of certain materials to minors.[6] It is, I feel, a testimonial to librarians as respected professionals that the courts do distinguish between materials that have been *selected* and those that are *available* in commercial outlets.

Now it must be noted that all the court cases I have referred to involved adolescents and it is not clear whether judges, at whatever level in the legal system, make a fundamental distinction between children and adolescents. The legal term *minors* encompasses everyone under the age of eighteen, and librarians would do well to remember that each time the Supreme Court has been faced with a case involving the right of young people to buy pornography or see an X-rated movie, it has denied free access.

Besides the battles being fought in the courts, a concern with the rights of children was being demonstrated by the publication of books on "children's liberation," and by special issues in numerous feminist magazines. John Holt in *Escape from Child-*

39

hood[7] offered a radical "bill of rights" for children that included the right to vote and all other rights guaranteed to adults. His chapter, "The Right to Control One's Learning," is essential reading for children's librarians, whether we agree with Holt or not.

Basically, Holt's approach to children's liberation involves the removal of external restraints from the lives of children. On the other hand, feminists and people concerned with racism (who may or may not be the same people) place their emphasis on removing the *internal* restraints that are imposed by social conditioning.

This is not to say that Holt would not like a world rid of racism and sexism, or that feminists and anti-racists would not welcome removal of many of the external restraints imposed upon children. The two views are found within the library profession, with the Office for Intellectual Freedom focusing on the legal aspects of freedom and the social responsibility librarians focusing on internal freedom. Of course, as within society as a whole, there are librarians who reject the entire concept of children's liberation whether legal or internal. These librarians see all liberation movements as undermining the established order of society, instead of as avenues to a better world.

Schizophrenia Within The Profession

Inserting the word *age* into the Library Bill of Rights did not magically provide young people with free access to library materials. In the five-year period between 1967 and 1972, so many questions arose that the ALA Intellectual Freedom Committee felt compelled to present to Council an interpretation of the issues, entitled "Free Access to Libraries for Minors."[8] (See *Intellectual Freedom Manual* for this and other official ALA policies on intellectual freedom.)

ALA's Association for Library Services to Children (then called CSD) provided what many saw as an example of professional schizophrenia when, at the June 1972 annual conference, its Board of Directors endorsed the ALA/IFC "Free Access to Libraries for Minors," *and* adopted a policy entitled "Statement on Reevaluation of Children's Materials" (See Appendix A). The negative reaction of the ALA/IFC to the latter action clearly took the CSD Board of Directors by surprise.

At the 1973 Midwinter meetings, the two groups met together and CSD amended its statement (see Appendix B). This action was still not entirely satisfactory to the ALA/IFC and eventually, the entire statement was rescinded in January 1976 following a presentation by Dianne Farrell to the CSD Board on behalf of CSD's Intellectual Freedom Committee (see Appendix C).

It is not my intention here to discuss the content of these statements or review the arguments made by both groups. What I want to do is identify the basic questions involved, even though I have no satisfactory answers. The questions are:

1. Should present selection standards prevent racist and sexist materials from being added to children's library collections?

2. If the answer to question 1 is yes, should those standards be applied to older titles that were written and purchased in a different social climate?

3. If children have free access to the entire collection, which in the adult department will contain many blatantly racist and sexist materials, is it a violation of children's rights to exclude such materials from the children's room?

My own emotional reactions to these questions are that I could live with excluding blatantly racist and sexist materials from the children's collection *if* the children have free access to the total library collection. At the same time, I recognize that this compromise would not be acceptable to many members of the library profession.

I find no difficulty in accepting Donnarae MacCann's distinction between materials that contribute to the cognitive development of a child and those that are attacks upon the child's emerging self-concept. According to the works of Jean Piaget, cognitive development in children proceeds in stages and children construct their own ideas about the nature of the world, ideas that are quite different from those held by the adults in

41

their lives. Cognitive development in Piaget's terms is the process of giving up erroneous ideas for more correct ideas about the nature of the world. For example, young children inevitably equate *bigger* with *heavier*, even though the small stone clearly outweighs an inflated balloon; they equate *bigger* with *more*, as every adult who has conned a young child into exchanging a dime for a nickel knows. In their own good time, children give up these erroneous ideas because they acquire enough experiences to allow them to make their own corrections. As adults, we can try all we want to tell children that *more* is not *bigger*, or *bigger* is not *heavier*. We can even force them to say they agree with us. But until they are ready to acquire those concepts as part of their internalized cognitive development, they secretly hold on to their own view of reality.

Self-concept, however, is not a cognitive process but an attitudinal one. All librarians, not just those working with children, should read Mary Ellen Goodman's *Race Awareness in Young Children*.[9] This study of four-year-olds' attitudes toward race was conducted in the 1940s and shows clearly that white four-year-olds never ask questions about their color—or lack of it. They take for granted that "white is right." Children of color—even those whose actual skin color is lighter than some of the children who are "white"—not only are aware of race but know that "the people that are brown—they have to go down."

Goodman's book was originally published in 1952 and she had already connected racism with sexism. She commented:

> Among Americans personal appearance is more stressed for girls than for boys. We find in our sample that girls appear among the high-awareness children more often than do boys. The connection between learning that personal appearance is important and taking note of racial appearance is demonstrated in this difference between girls and boys as well as in the difference between Negroes and whites.[10]

However much I would like to be an intellectual freedom purist, I cannot read about four-year-olds who already understand that they are second-class citizens and want to contribute to the continuance of that type of social conditioning. I cannot read all the research studies that show how little adult women think of themselves and other women without feeling that the sort of social conditioning that limits options and leads to self-hate must stop somewhere, and where better to stop than in childhood!

It should be clear by now that I think the Council on Interracial Books for Children is wrong in lumping materialism and elitism in with racism and sexism. Each time an ism is added to the list, the entire concept becomes harder to defend. Moreover, some of the isms conflict. One may argue long into the night about the values/horrors of materialism in the abstract, but the fact remains that many victims of racism and sexism are poor people who would like to have a nice apartment, good furniture, modern appliances, and other material advantages. "Materialism" seems an inadequate description of their problem.

Of all the isms the Council worries about, elitism is the most difficult to deal with in our present society. Most of us know that there is a double standard—children from lower-class homes are subjected to more stringent codes of behavior in schools, libraries, and society in general than are middle-class children. A prank in a middle-class neighborhood is treated as a prank; in a lower-class neighborhood it can get the child shot or locked up. Those are the facts of life in our society. Elitism is shown in all its viciousness in Richard Peck's *Are You in the House Alone?* [11] where the adolescent rapist comes from the town's "best family" and that protects him from justice. But when the Council labels Kin Platt's *Headman* [12] "elitist" because the central character becomes a gang leader, it misrepresents elitism. We will probably never arrive at a time when all human beings possess identical qualities. Some will always lead and some will follow; some will be good at one task and some good at another. Elitism is wrong, in my opinion, when it is institutionalized as a class privilege or when some people are deprived of the opportunity to do whatever they can do best.

On the other hand, we should not confuse civil liberties with social conditioning. One can defend the former without contributing to the transmission of attitudes that wrap people in such stereotypes that they are unable to be free in any genuine sense of the word. This point of view is reflected in the resolution passed by ALA Council in July 1976 (see Appendix D) which calls upon librarians and the profession as a whole to initiate programs that contribute to increased awareness of racism and sexism on the part of librarians and members of the public.

An analysis of the censorship attacks upon schools and libraries as reported in the *Newsletter on Intellectual Freedom* shows that many, if not most, cases have as their basis the racist or sexist attitudes held by the would-be censors. Perhaps the most dramatic proof of this was found in the Kanawha County (West Virginia) controversy over the use of multi-ethnic textbooks. The report prepared by a special committee of the National Education Association stated:

> Spokespersons for the anti-book movement vigorously denied that there was any element of racism in their protest or in their community—except, they alleged, in the "racial hatred" portrayed in the books. If the protest movement and the community itself are as free from racial prejudice as its leaders claim, then Kanawha County, West Virginia, is indeed unique among all the counties in this country. And if the protest is as free from racism as its leaders claim, then it is difficult to understand why teachers have received complaints from parents about illustrations in textbooks depicting a white female student and a black male student together. Or why a minister was called by an irate parent who wanted to know if the minister wanted his daughter to marry a black man. Or why some members of the Citizens Textbook Review Committee who recommended retention of the books received numerous telephone calls that they described as obscene and, in almost all instances, dealing with race. Or why, as reported to the Panel, a building in an outlying area of the county was painted with lettering that stated, "Get the nigger books out!" [13]

All of us have vested professional interests, as well as personal and societal interests, in lessening the level of racism found in our society. The question is whether *libraries as institutions* should take steps to help society achieve that goal. This question was never asked at the time when libraries as institutions devoted their energies mainly to reinforcing the value system of the white middle class, a fact that may offer a clue as to the degree of racism within the library profession.

A parallel dilemma is found within the health professions, where the old established view was that the proper role of health professionals was to cure illness. Today, within the health sciences, there is a social responsibility group that maintains that the proper role of health professionals lies in *preventing* illness. The two groups manage to coexist, though not in perfect harmony, and there may be a message therein for librarians. Perhaps we can agree that the children's collection can serve as the preventive clinic for racism while leaving the curative role to other library departments.

Only one thing is certain in all this: there will be no unanimity within the profession, or even within one library. The problem is too complex for a simple answer or for everyone to arrive at the same answer. The important point is that all of us should think through our own positions on the subject—and respect other people's right to reach different conclusions.

NOTES FOR CHAPTER 3

1. Richard Peck, *Are You in the House Alone?* New York: Viking, 1976.
2. "Old Values Surface in Blume Country," *Interracial Books for Children Bulletin*, vol. 7, no, 5, 1976, pp. 8–10.
3. Donnarae MacCann, "Children's Books in a Pluralistic Society," *Wilson Library Bulletin*, October 1976, pp. 154–62.
4. For an overview of court cases and legal rights of youth, *see* articles by Pamela Evelyn Procuniar and Eileen Sullivan in *Wilson Library Bulletin*, October 1976.
5. For the complete text of the Strongsville decision, see *School Library Journal*, November 1976, pp. 23–7.
6. Ginzberg v New York, 390 U.S. 629 (1968).
7. John Holt, *Escape from Childhood: The Needs and Rights of Childhood*, New York: Ballantine Bks, 1975.
8. "Free Access to Libraries for Minors," see *Intellectual Freedom Manual*, Chicago: American Library Association, 1974.
9. Mary Ellen Goodman *Race Awareness in Young Children*, New York: Collier Bks, 1964 [c. 1952], pp. 50–62.
10. *Ibid.*, p. 205.
11. Peck, *op. cit.*
12. Kin Platt, *Headman*, New York: Greenwillow Bks, 1975.
13. *Kanawha County, West Virginia: A Textbook Study in Cultural Conflict*, Washington, DC: Natl. Educ. Assn., 1975, p. 41.

CHAPTER FOUR

Sex and Sexuality in Children's Books

LIBRARIANS who work with children, whether in public libraries or elementary schools, have more trouble with sex education materials than with any other category of materials they buy. They also receive less help in selecting such materials because there are no clear guidelines available in library literature. Some librarians avoid the problem by not buying any but the most innocuous sex education materials; other librarians buy the best books but keep them locked up. In most parts of North America, it still takes genuine courage on the part of a librarian to buy forthright sex education materials and give them shelf space, accessible to all.

Most of us would agree that librarians have a responsibility to buy and make easily available the best sex education books written for children. We would also probably agree that children who want information on sex have as much right to receive it as children who want information on hockey rules. In fact, however, sex and sexuality are not seen by many adults as proper subjects for children to explore. Not only have we as a society been reluctant to help our children to reach a rational understanding of these subjects, but we have also avoided finding out what knowledge of sex they may have gained without our help. Thus, Jean Piaget, who explored all kinds of children's thought patterns, drew the line when it came to sex. He wrote in *The*

47

Child's Conception of the World (first published in English in 1929):

> ... it would be well to know children's ideas on the birth of babies. But it goes without saying that there are grave moral and pedagogic reasons for not pursuing such an investigation directly. [1]

The fact that Piaget could use the phrase "it goes without saying" suggests how deeply ingrained this taboo is in our society. It is still impossible in the last quarter of the twentieth century to conceive of most researchers exploring sex and sexuality with children. We must, then, constantly remind ourselves that we know very little of the ways in which children think about sex.

By indirect means, such as studying children's conversations, Piaget discovered that young children's questions about birth suggest two different levels of awareness. On the first level, children who ask the "where did I come from?" question assume that they existed prior to their arrival in the family and only want to know the circumstances of their arrival. This level of awareness is satisfied by answers that involve being brought by a stork or being found on the doorstep or under a cabbage.

An old joke acquires new meaning in this context. A little boy came home from school and asked excitedly, "Mother, where did I come from?" The mother, who had been waiting for the day this question would be asked, plunged into a lengthy explanation of how a baby is conceived and born. At the end, the boy said, "Yes, Mommy, but where did I come from? The new girl in our class comes from Kansas."

There is, however, a second level of awareness in which children asking this very same question really require a serious answer about how life begins. Children at this level of awareness have some recognition that their birth is the direct result of something their parents have done. In other words, they have a glimmering that being born is part of a cause-and-effect relationship. [2]

As librarians we must direct ourselves toward providing materials that answer the second and deeper awareness when we encounter the "where did I come from?" question.

CRITERIA FOR EVALUATING BOOKS FOR YOUNG CHILDREN

Books for young children (preschoolers through primary grades) on sex education are written on the assumption that all children, sooner or later, will want to know where they came from. We have no idea, actually, what percentage of children ask this question of their parents. (An informal survey of my generation provoked as the usual response, "I wouldn't have dared ask!") Nor do we know what percentage of parents feel the need to explain the birth process even if the question has not been asked. What we do know is that for the parents of children who do ask, and for those parents who feel the need to explain, help is needed in answering and good books are essential.

Criteria for evaluating books for any age group come in two types: attitudinal and informational. Both types of criteria grow in complexity with the age of the intended audience.

For young children, a good book on sex education should convey two essential attitudes. First, the sexual act that leads to a baby being created should be connected with the human emotions of love, tenderness, and commitment between the man and woman. Second, the book should convey the idea, either implicitly or explicitly, that having a baby is a conscious decision on the part of the parents. In a world that desperately needs population control, the idea that babies are inevitable is harmful. Traditionally, authors have always been very good about stressing the attitude of "we chose you" in books for adopted children, but have rarely considered whether this attitude might not be just as important for biologically produced children to receive. The children we serve today are going to grow up in a world where having babies will not be seen as an inevitable outcome of marriage or any other committed relationship between women and men. We will do them a great favor by not teaching them otherwise.

What is the minimum information a good book offers? The following criteria represent the basic facts:

1. A male (father) and a female (mother) are necessary for conception to occur.

2. The male contributes sperm and the female contributes an egg and they (male-female, egg-sperm) must meet.

3. The process by which they meet is called sexual intercourse or "making love."

4. That process involves the male's penis coming to a state of erection so that it can enter the female's vagina.

5. There must be clear anatomical illustrations showing the location of the penis and vagina in relationship to the total body, so that such vague phrases as "the man enters the woman" cannot be misconstrued to mean a finger in the ear or something equally erroneous.

6. The growth of the fetus in the mother's womb should be described—the amount of detail may vary, but the process should be made clear.

7. The birth of the baby should also be explained; again, the amount of detail may vary.

A Questionable Approach

It is highly debatable whether the use of nonhuman analogies in sex education books is relevant to children's needs or, in fact, understandable to children. The discussion of how puppies, kittens, chickens, or flowers are reproduced may make some adults more comfortable with the ultimate question of how "big people" reproduce, but there is evidence that such analogies only serve to confuse children. The children we are talking about here fall into what Piaget calls "The Preoperational Subperiod" (ages 2–7) and one of the characteristics of that group is "irreversibility."

Adults take for granted their ability to operate "reversibly" and probably do not remember the time when they did not think this way. This makes it difficult for us to understand how complex a thought process reversibility actually is. In *The Origins of Intellect: Piaget's Theory*, Phillips offers us the following example:

A four-year-old subject is asked:
"Do you have a brother?" He says, "Yes."
"What's his name?" "Jim."
"Does Jim have a brother?" "No." [3]

Clearly children who cannot make this type of "reverse" connection are unlikely to see what animal behavior patterns have to do
with human behavior.

Another objection to the use of animals falls into the category
of attitude conveyance. One highly praised book, *How Babies
Are Made,* [4] uses animals in the early pages. The rooster is shown
on top of the hen; the male dog on top of the bitch. Then, when
it comes to man and woman, they are covered by a blanket. Such
a book serves to reinforce the idea that sexual relationships between human beings must be "covered up." They *are* private,
but that is an entirely different matter.

Euphemisms

Euphemisms for body parts or sexual acts are to be avoided.
Correct terms should be applied to all anatomical organs and all
behavior. This is not much of a problem in modern books, but
older ones still being recommended do contain imprecise language. In *The Story of a Baby,* for example, Marie Hall Ets refers
constantly to "the stuff of life." [5] In an older book from England,
happily not found in many libraries, called *Peter and Caroline,*
the mother describes a penis to her son by saying, "You have a
little thing, as big as a finger, to wee with." [6]

Some parents undoubtedly do talk to their own children in
euphemisms and cute terms, but the tone is not useful in a book.
Books are for providing clear and objective information.

Especially to be watched is the phrase "the fetus grows in the
mother's tummy." Just as the vagueness of phrases like "the man
enters the woman" can be destructive to children's understanding of what we are trying to tell them, so substituting the
"tummy" for the womb confuses the function of digestion with
that of birth.

Parents should be identified as fathers and mothers and not as
husbands and wives. Marriage is not essential to procreation and
has no business being introduced into a biological discussion.
Aside from the basic truth of that statement, we should recognize that many children are born out of wedlock and they have a
right to an explanation of birth unencumbered by considerations
that do not apply to them.

Religion and Sex

Many people are concerned that most of the newer sex education books do not stress religious concepts in their discussion of birth or the relationship between women and men. I will have more to say on this in discussing books for older children, because at that level there is a problem. For young children, however, the birth process we are trying to explain is an abstraction. To complicate that explanation with a further abstraction—religion—is not good pedagogic sense. Again, as Piaget has observed, "The religious instruction imparted to children between the ages of 4 and 7 often appears as something foreign to the child's natural thought."[7] It is far more important that books stress concepts of love and caring, which are, after all, concepts young children can understand.

Problem Areas

We have been talking so far about books that help answer the basic question of where babies come from. There are a number of good ones available today. What we do not have are books that distinguish between sexual intercourse, which is a physical activity, and sexuality, which all of us have from birth to the grave even if we never engage in sexual intercourse. And it may be that children's real need is not simply to understand the act of two adults that gave them birth but rather to understand their own feelings and potential.

While it is true that we have little valid research into the sexual feelings of children, certain observations can be made from personal experience. All of us who have watched young children in uninhibited environments know that they enjoy touching their genitals. Clearly, this touching gives them pleasure and what seems at issue is how to teach them that there comes an age when such pleasure should be achieved in private, which is not the same as in secret. There probably will never come a time when all adults will agree that this activity is per se acceptable. One hopes, however, that there will come a time when most adults are comfortable enough with their own sexuality not to be frightened by its presence in children.

There will certainly come a time in most children's lives when they explore each other's bodies. Our society calls this activity "playing doctor and nurse," although just why it is not called "doctor and patient" is a mystery. Touching oneself or exploring another's body is an expression of sexuality, and children should be granted that freedom of expression without being made to feel guilty.

As a small beginning in this area, books that deal with the five senses might go on to observe that it feels good to touch our own bodies. Librarians must begin to think about these matters now because it will not be long before we are faced with the problem of evaluating dozens of books that try to convey sexuality to young children. The publication in 1975 of *Show Me!*[8] is but a harbinger of things to come. Its huge popular success practically guarantees that others will follow.

There is so much wrong with *Show Me!* that it would require an entire chapter to detail. In the present context, I want to point out that the emphasis on adult sexual behavior in the photographs is a denial of the book's purported aim of helping young children understand their own sexuality. The captions accompanying the photographs emphasize the most negative attitudes toward sex. The text in the back of the book (as opposed to the captions) is directed at adults and is strangely at variance with the message the photographs are supposedly conveying.

Until *Show Me!* appeared, it was possible to observe that sexism was merely implicit in sex education books for young children. With *Show Me!* the implicit became explicit. The text makes it very clear that mothers have the primary responsibility for rearing children; that they must breast-feed their children or be prepared to have them grow up to be neurotic and antisocial; and that a mother who does not devote all of the first year and most of the next four to being with her child is a thoughtless, cruel creature.

Implicit sexism in older books takes a number of forms. Of forty titles examined before writing this analysis, only one, Peter Mayle's *Where Did I Come From?*[9] assigned female gender to the fetus despite the fact that fifty per cent of births do produce female children. All books, including Mayle's, showed only male doctors, although Mayle did define the doctor as "mother's little helper" which suggests that it is the mother and not the doctor who is the primary agent in the birth process.

The books that I label as "cute" are the worst offenders in perpetuating sexism. They are the books written as a running conversation between mother and son. It is interesting to note that while the myth prevails that fathers and sons are expected to have man-to-man talks about sex, the cute books always have the mother doing the explaining—and always to a son, never a daughter. Worst of all, the son always finds his mother in the kitchen. A stunning example of sexism plus the worst in cute writing is *Johnny Jack and His Beginnings* by Pearl Buck. [10]

BOOKS FOR OLDER CHILDREN

An interesting phenomenon in juvenile publishing is that while one finds sex education books both for young children and for those of junior high school age, there is precious little available for the nine-to-twelve-year-old group. One possible reason for this situation is that until recently most of our energies were directed toward sex information rather than education for sexuality. We have unconsciously assumed that once young children have learned where babies come from, there is no interest in sex and sexuality until they reach the stage where adolescent growth patterns make sexual activity a real possibility.

One reflection of this attitude can be found in *An Introduction to Children's Work in Public Libraries*, where, over a decade ago, I could write about the appropriateness of subject matter to age level by saying, "This means that a novel about teen-age marriage is not appropriate for a children's room regardless of how immature its treatment of the subject may be. Such books are best bought for young adult collections where the problem is a real one to the potential reader." [11] The suggestion in my statement that problems of sex and marriage were not likely to be encountered before young adulthood was probably never true for all children, but it seemed to be true for the majority at the time. The same cannot be said today. We know from Planned Parenthood clinics that children as young as ten are coming for counseling *after* they have become sexually active. We know from the statistics that there is a large increase in the number of pre-teen females giving birth and that the single greatest medical problem among youth is venereal disease. In such an environment it seems essential that authors and publishers should direct more energy to producing good books for the nine-to-twelve-year-olds.

When such books are written they must contain all the information found in books for younger children. Authors must not assume a foundation of existing knowledge to build upon but start from the beginning. They must then add new knowledge by discussing menstruation and the fertility cycle in women. Without unduly complicated discussion, the authors should tell children that females are born with all the eggs they are ever going to produce but that males do not, ordinarily, have sperm until they reach adolescence.

It would be appropriate at this age to introduce genetics by explaining that the male's sperm carries the chromosome that will determine the sex of the baby to be born. A lengthy explanation is not needed, but since some idea of genetics is important in sex education books for older age groups, a beginning should be made early. An understanding of sex determination of the fetus is important, indeed vital. Henry VIII is not the only man in history who changed wives to sire a son, and it is necessary for males to accept the fact that they provide the sex determinant chromosome. At the same time, the genetic approach should help both males and females to understand that male potency is not an issue when the baby is female.

Older children need a very clear explanation of how the male's penis serves both for urination and for sexual activity, but that both cannot occur at the same time. They need a clear anatomical drawing that shows that women have both a urethra and a vagina, the former being for urination and the latter for sexual penetration. This difference between male and female anatomy causes major problems for both sexes if it is not clearly understood.

While accurate information related in a way that upper elementary and junior high school children can understand is vital, even more important are books that discuss the decision to become sexually active. Everyone working in a counseling situation with young people agrees that it is easier for anyone to remain sexually inactive than to stop being active once started.

Experts have identified three reasons that the young (from ten up) become sexually active. Some simply are endowed with a higher sex urge than most people are, and in such children the urge to participate in sexual activity seems to surface earlier as well. For these children, the best we can do is make sure that pregnancy and venereal disease do not result. Clinic workers have learned to accept the fact that they cannot change these children's sexual behavior patterns; the rest of us would do well to adopt a similar attitude.

A second reason for children becoming sexually active is social pressure. This is sometimes referred to as peer pressure but that is too limiting—the correct term is social pressure. Both girls and boys feel the pressure that comes from television shows and commercials, from movies, and from magazine advertisements that exploit sex; girls may experience pressure from mothers who buy them "training bras" before their breasts have developed; boys may experience pressure from the attitude that defines masculinity by sexual prowess. Girls raised in a sexist atmosphere experience the further pressure of having been taught that women are only defined in relationship to men and begin as early as possible to have a male companion. When one adds to all these adult-induced pressures the fact that some children will have peers who enjoy being sexually active, the pressure can become intolerable. Some of these children who have become sexually active because of social pressure go to a clinic looking for support and approval in ceasing their sexual activity. Others come to a clinic before any major sexual experience in hope of finding a way to postpone sexual activity. These girls and boys do not need moralistic lectures—they need to be able to find sources in society that tell them frankly that they have a *right* to delay sexual activity. They need sources that tell them that they are not weird or abnormal if they decide to wait a few years for sexual experience.

Finally, there are children who engage in sexual activity to defy their parents or adult society in general. These children really need professional therapy to help them understand the antagonism they are feeling. The most that books can do is to plant in their minds the idea that hurting oneself is a poor way of "getting even" with someone else. People of any age with this motivation have never developed that inner sense of self that lets them see themselves as persons of worth without external references. Books are unlikely to penetrate that lack of self acceptance although it is always worth trying to spell out what is at issue.

BOOKS FOR JUNIOR HIGH SCHOOL AGE YOUTH

Until good books for children of upper elementary school age become available, we must rely upon the best of the books produced for junior high school students or young adolescents. Besides giving information on human reproduction, these books now discuss four topics that were totally ignored in books prior to the 1960s: (1) birth control, (2) masturbation, (3) venereal disease, and (4) homosexuality. Some of the books also discuss abortion, but that topic is more often reserved for older adolescents.

Any discussion of birth control information for young people must begin by reminding the reader that until the women's movement of the last decade began to tell women that they had a right to sexual satisfaction without fear of pregnancy, society had decreed that pregnancy was a just punishment for women who indulged in sex outside of marriage. (There are still many people who believe this and they are the most vocal opponents of sex education in the schools.) Until the 1960s, doctors were forbidden by most state laws to give birth control information to unmarried women. In Canada, it was not until 1969 that birth control information could be disseminated publicly.

That we now find the subject of birth control acceptable for junior high school students is an indication that responsible adults realize that the very least we can do for young people is to keep their sexual activity from producing unwanted children or from forcing young women into the trauma of abortion. Earlier books took the point of view that sexual activity outside of marriage was never to be condoned and, if it took place, pregnancy was the price to be paid. The combination of pressure for population control and the women's movement accounts for some of this attitudinal change. A third factor, clear to anyone who has examined the statistics, is that younger and younger children are

57

engaging in sexual activity. In 1970, 44 percent of the illegitimate births in Canada were to mothers between the ages of 15 and 19. Not only are young mothers ill equipped to be supportive parents, but, as current medical statistics show, they also give birth to more defective children.

Children's librarians may feel that birth control information is inappropriate in books found in the children's room, but we have to keep in mind that those books may be very important to that minute percentage of ten-to-twelve-year-olds who are sexually active. The information cannot hurt those who do not need it, but it can ward off personal tragedy for someone who does need it.

Negative attitudes toward masturbation have been virulent in their intensity and primarily directed toward males. Young people were threatened with the fear that they would become insane, that their penises would fall off, or that they would become criminals. So taboo was the subject of masturbation that it never appeared in earlier sex education books. All these myths arose because observers in mental institutions and prisons saw the inmates masturbating. These observers, being untrained in research methods, concluded that masturbation *caused* insanity or criminal activities. They did not reason that people removed from all ordinary avenues of sexual intercourse might turn to masturbation for relief. As attitudes toward sex have changed in our society, authors of books on sex education now find it possible to inform young readers that masturbation is an acceptable sexual activity. That ordinary people who are neither insane nor criminal engage in it as an alternative to sexual frustration is an important message.

Venereal disease affects both sexes equally. The increase in venereal disease among the young has been so great that some states have passed laws protecting the confidentiality between doctors and patients in order to encourage young people to seek help without having their parents notified. Since treatment is more important than condemnation, good books describe the symptoms, warn of the dangerous effects without using scare techniques, and advise readers to seek immediate medical help.

Of the four topics, the most difficult one to deal with for

young readers is homosexuality. Authors are still struggling to find a way to describe homosexuality in a way that presents it as an acceptable sexual life for the minority without appearing to encourage it. If we look at the problem in relationship to the dilemma authors faced in the presentation of premarital sexual relationships in earlier times, we may gain some understanding of the problem. In the days when all books had to assume the stance that heterosexual relationships took place only within marriage, the authors conformed, even though the most perceptive writers understood that a marriage license had nothing to do with sexual desire or its satisfaction. Today, perceptive authors are trying to tell young people, both straight and gay, that while most people grow up heterosexual, a certain minority in every civilization grow up homosexual. The authors want to help heterosexual youths accept the sexual proclivity of their homosexual acquaintances and to affirm for the homosexual youths their right to their own life—all without appearing to "condone" or "encourage" homosexuality.

The problem of homosexuality as a topic for presentation to junior high school age youth is complicated by the fact that this is the time of life when many young people do have a sexual encounter with a member of the same sex. Most of the young people having a homosexual encounter will develop as heterosexuals, without guilt for having experienced the same-sex pleasure if adults do not overreact. For a small minority, this same-sex encounter in early adolescence will be so "right" that they will know this is for them.

Since the treatment of homosexuality varies greatly from book to book, it is worth our time to identify a few of the specific problems inherent in dealing with the subject. Authors like to ask the question; "What causes homosexuality?" No one knows the answer to that question, since we do not even know why most people grow up heterosexual. Unhappily, most authors, after admitting that no one knows the answer, then go on to expound whatever theory pleases them most. Close attention to an author's "explanation" will enable us to identify his or her particular bias.

Another indication of the author's bias can be found in the location of material on homosexuality. If it is treated with sado-masochism, child molestation, and other extreme psycho-sexual disorders, then the chances are the author is strongly biased against homosexuals.

Most authors recognize that the fear of homosexuality seems to haunt many adolescent males. In such books as Chartham's *Older Teenagers' Sex Questions Answered*[12] we can come to understand how deep-seated this fear is, mostly because the subject is surrounded by such horrendous myths about what kind of people homosexuals are.

The time to give young people a sense of perspective on the subject is in late elementary school grades—before they find themselves needing the information and before the myths become set in their minds. One myth that does more damage than any erroneous statement about homosexuality per se is that young people worried about homosexuality should go and talk to their family doctor or minister. Until the early 1970s, most medical schools offered no information on sexuality for potential doctors. Doctors were taught the biological facts of sex but nothing about the psychology of sexuality. Most ministers or priests were not even taught the facts, much less theories, of sexuality. Any book suggesting that troubled young people turn to these professionals for help should, at the very least, carry a warning that not all doctors or ministers are better qualified than other people to give advice on the matter.

In summary, the message that all sex education books should convey, from early childhood through adulthood, is that sexual relationships are *one way* in which two people who care about each other demonstrate that caring. People may have sex without caring; people may care for each other without having sex together, but when two people genuinely care for each other, their sex life is their own business.

It is absolutely essential that all sex education materials stress the caring, the tenderness, the love between the people having sex together. And while the books will talk about the pleasure experienced, and rightly so, they must not stress one person's pleasure but emphasize the mutuality. Only then can authors make clear that exploitive sex—whether homosexual or heterosexual—is the only kind that is morally wrong.

60

NOTES FOR CHAPTER 4

1. Jean Piaget, *The Child's Conception of the World*, translated by Joan and Andrew Tomlinson, Totowa, NJ: Rowman & Littlefield, 1960, p. 360.
2. *Ibid*, p. 361.
3. John L. Phillips, Jr., *The Origins of Intellect: Piaget's Theory*, San Francisco: Freeman, 1969, p. 61.
4. Andrew C. Andry, and Steven Shepp, *How Babies Are Made*, illustrated by Blake Hamptom, New York: Time-Life, 1968, n.p.
5. Marie Hall Ets, *The Story of a Baby*, New York: Viking, 1939.
6. Sten Hegeler, *Peter and Caroline: A Child Asks About Childbirth and Sex*, translated by Maurice Michael, London: Tavistock Publications, 1957, p. 5.
7. Piaget, *op. cit.*, p. 353.
8. Will McBride, *Show Me! A Picture Book of Sex for Children and Parents*, New York: St. Martin's, 1975.
9. Peter Mayle, *Where Did I Come From?* illustrated by Arthur Robins, New York: Lyle Stuart, 1973.
10. Pearl Buck, *Johnny Jack and His Beginnings*, New York: John Day, 1954.
11. Dorothy M. Broderick, *An Introduction to Children's Work in Public Libraries*, New York: H. W. Wilson, 1965, pp. 30-1.
12. Robert Chartham, *Older Teenagers' Sex Questions Answered*, London: Corgi Books, 1973.

CHAPTER
FIVE

The Selection Process

THE SELECTION process is the application of the standards that we have established to actual materials available for purchase. This chapter will look first at the selection of books and then at audiovisual materials.

BOOKS

It is often said that ideally we should put no book on the shelf that we have not read. This ideal often creates resentment—who has *that* much time?—or despair, leading us not even to try since the accomplishment is so far removed from the ideal.

Neither reaction is necessary if we stop to examine where and how the ideal arose. Large metropolitan systems with a headquarters staff and many children's or school librarians in branches or schools do not have to rely on outside aids for book selection decisions. These systems receive review copies of new books and the books are read and evaluated by members of the staff. Such a system can say quite accurately that no book is bought unless it has been read. However, that statement really means that no book has been bought that has not been read by *someone on the staff*, which is a very different statement.

Within many states this ideal is becoming more easily attainable by librarians in small towns as the concept of cooperative library systems spreads. The system can join the Greenaway Plan, which automatically provides prepublication copies of all new titles from certain publishers. The librarian in the small, independent library then has the opportunity of attending monthly meetings of the system's members at which books are discussed and evaluated as well as displayed. Alternatively, a system can produce a review list of new titles and send the actual books around to the member libraries. There is no question that one of the biggest advantages of a cooperative library system is the possibility of actually seeing a book before buying it. However informative reviews may be, nothing quite takes the place of firsthand evaluation.

One advantage in having a local reviewer is that we can call up the person and ask questions about the book if the review contains ambiguities. It is possible to ask, "What did you mean by that?" instead of writing an irate letter to the book review editor *after* the purchase.

In the United States there are examination centers where librarians and teachers can go to look at and read new books. Librarians in the New York area can use the Children's Book Council collection. The center I am most familiar with is at the University of Wisconsin—Madison. It employs a professional librarian who has fulltime clerical help plus student assistants. The center does more than offer the opportunity to see new books. It plans programs that bring authors, illustrators, and editors to Madison to talk about children's books. It celebrates special occasions, such as Children's Book Week, and encourages visits from school classes. It is also helpful to students doing research in children's literature.

It costs money to run a good examination center, but if we believe in the need for good quality children's books in our libraries, we should be willing to seek monetary support for such centers.

However we work out the book selection process, we should try to make it a group activity. Where no systems exist, or where no examination centers are within reach, we should try to organize a congenial group of librarians who can meet regularly and discuss the books we have already bought on the basis of reviews. This not only has the advantage of familiarizing us with the content of the books but can also alert us to differences between our values and the values of the original reviewer.

Cooperation is important for two reasons: first, it is easier and more enjoyable to make decisions in a social atmosphere; second, it helps keep personal prejudices in line. All of us have blind spots—subjects that do not interest us, types of books that do not appeal to us—and when selection is done in total isolation, these prejudices tend to influence our decisions despite our best intentions.

Guidelines

It used to be possible to advise people buying children's books that there was no rush. This is no longer true. If we want a hardback book, it is important to buy it as soon as it is published. Economic conditions are forcing publishers to let books go out of print sooner than they used to. It came as a distinct shock to me to discover that the Clara Ingram Judson biographies were out of print in the spring of 1976. So if you are determined to have a hardback collection, buy quickly. And pray for an economic upswing.

The portion of the materials budget designated for books should be divided in three parts to pay for original hardbacks, replacement titles, and paperbacks.

Paperbacks

Paperbacks have been accepted reluctantly by librarians, yet the time may be coming when the majority of books in our collections will be paperbacks. Certainly, children would rather borrow them. Paperbacks are less expensive than hardbacks; they take up less space; and many books are now available only in a paper format.

All libraries should be on the mailing lists of paperback publishers. Every major paperback house now puts out a catalog of its titles for various age groups, and these catalogs are invaluable. Some of the paperback houses also provide promotional materials. Dell did a superb poster for its science-fiction titles; Avon has produced a free cassette on which Norma Klein talks about *Mom, the Wolfman and Me,* Richard Peck discusses *Dreamland Lake,* and Alice Childress talks about *A Hero Ain't Nothing But a Sandwich.*

Just as it has taken librarians a long time to recognize the potential of paperbacks, so it has taken paperback houses a long time to recognize the market potential of libraries. The major paperback houses now have library promotion people just as the hardcover houses do, and these promotion people can be helpful when we have trouble with local paperback distributors.

Replacement Titles

Replacements are probably the heart of a library collection. In public libraries there is an entirely new clientele every eight years; in elementary school libraries, the turnover is every six years, if the school does not have a kindergarten. Children should not be penalized because they were born thirty or forty or fifty years after such standards as *Mr. Popper's Penguins, Millions of Cats,* or *The Story About Ping* were published.

There really is a right time for reading some books. I have watched a ten-year-old friend of mine laugh himself silly over *Stuart Little,* and much as I enjoy the book, I know that I do not come near experiencing his joy. In telling stories to children, or participating in preschool programs, I am never able to anticipate fully the high level of children's delight in the old favorites, the classics that their parents probably enjoyed years before.

Building a Collection

The tools discussed in this section serve to help us decide what books to replace. They can also aid in planning a new collection. These and other tools useful in this process will be found in the bibliography at the end of this book.

The two giants among selection aids are Bro-Dart's *Elementary School Library Collection* (called *Bro-Dart* for short) and the *Children's Catalog.* Both cover all the major divisions found in the Dewey Decimal system. *Bro-Dart* contains approximately three times as many titles as *Children's Catalog,* and has the added advantage of listing audiovisual materials and adult professional tools and periodicals.

Bro-Dart is revised annually, and certainly a school or public library undertaking a complete evaluation of a large collection would do well to use it. It has the added benefit of being the product of a commercial processor, so that materials listed in it can be ordered from Bro-Dart and will arrive at the library fully cataloged. It has taken librarians a long time to realize that the cost of commercial processing is a valid expense, freeing the library's professional staff for service functions.

For librarians working with smaller collections, *Children's Catalog* may be the more appropriate tool. A completely revised edition is published every five years, and annual supplements are issued between editions. A library that owned all the books listed in the *Catalog* would have made a good start toward assembling a well-rounded collection of reasonable quality.

Public librarians working in library systems that consider children's collections to run through the eighth grade, and elementary school librarians whose clientele warrants extensive purchase of junior high school materials, will want to consult *Junior High School Catalog,* as well.

Because children's books are going out of print so rapidly these days, *Bro-Dart* and *Children's Catalog* should be used in conjunction with *Children's Books in Print* and *Paperback Books in Print. Subject Guide to Children's Books in Print* is also extremely useful. If, in checking a library's holdings against one or the other of the standard bibliographies, we identify areas of weakness in the collection, we should note the publication dates of the books recommended. If they are nonfiction titles, the *Subject Guide* should be consulted to see if newer titles are available.

While the practice of ordering books from publishers' catalogs is unacceptable when acquiring new titles, it is acceptable when selecting replacements. Most publishers now put out catalogs that include their back titles and indicate standard bibliographies that list the books. Knowledgeable librarians can work very well from these catalogs and should be grateful for the work the publishing houses have saved them.

Checking the library's holdings against the *Children's Catalog* should be done at least every five years. (If you are new to the library, it should be one of your first tasks.) At first glance, this seems a tedious chore, but it is the best way to know the collection we are working with. Weaknesses in the collection will be identified and alert us that either we or our predecessors had blind spots when it came to developing a balanced collection.

There are some librarians who, when they discover that a standard work is not in their collection, rationalize its absence by claiming to own other books on the subject. This is spurious reasoning, since it is not the number of books we own on a subject but the quality of the books that determines how good the collection is. Only after we own the best books on a subject should we begin to fill in with what is termed "additional material." ("Additional materials" are those that meet the minimum standard we have established for that particular category of book and are bought to satisfy heavy user demand.)

User demand that cannot be met is another clue to weaknesses in the collection. If a child asks for a book on model airplanes or how to repair a bicycle and we discover we do not own a book on the topic, *Subject Guide to Children's Books in Print* will tell us what is available on the subject and *Bro-Dart* or the *Children's Catalog* will identify the best books on the subject. All unfulfilled requests for books should be kept on file, preferably on three-by-five cards, and material on the subjects should be ordered as soon as possible. Some school systems have established time periods when orders may be placed; others allow the librarian to order any time throughout the year.

Another helpful tool in book selection is *The Best in Children's Books*, edited by Zena Sutherland, which is the successor to *Good Books for Children*, edited by Mary K. Eakin. It covers 1,400 books recommended between 1966 and 1972 by *The Bulletin of the Center for Children's Books* at the University of Chicago. Since it is arranged by author, each entry being numbered, the indexes are an important part of the work. It is particularly useful to school librarians, who are often called upon to provide materials for values education. If a school were considering instituting a family-life program, the many subject headings, such as "Father-daughter relations," "Father-son relations," etc., would prove extremely useful. It is the only tool that indexes human values in books as well as factual content.

The staff of *School Library Journal* annually compile *Best Books for Children,* which contains over 4,000 titles. It is divided by grade levels and within grade levels by subject. There are brief annotations for those books whose titles do not make their content obvious.

Used judiciously, the bibliographies described above can meet the needs of all but the largest collections of children's books. For in-depth collection building in specific areas, however, there are many specialized bibliographies. Perhaps the best known of these is the *AAAS Children's Book List.* This consists entirely of science books and is published by the American Association for the Advancement of Science. This cooperative effort between scientists and librarians has set a high standard for cooperative projects. The scientists have the factual knowledge to evaluate the content of the books and the librarians relate the books to the needs and interests of children.

As more and more emphasis is placed on meeting the needs of children whose first language is Spanish, librarians will be called upon to provide materials that are in Spanish and that reflect Hispanic culture. An example of a tool that can be helpful in this area is *Bilingual-Bicultural Materials: A Listing for Library Resource Centers,* compiled by staff members of the El Paso (Texas) public schools. This bibliography has the advantage of informing us whether the item under review is recommended for first, second, or third purchase, or not recommended at all. Besides covering books and traditional audiovisual materials, *Bilingual-Bicultural Materials* evaluates games. It is an excellent example of how a single school system can make a nationwide contribution.

What is important for all of us to remember is that whatever our needs, the chances are that someone has already done a bibliography that we can use as a starting point. These bibliographies may never be reviewed, but, since they are relatively inexpensive, when we see them listed in news items or in columns devoted to "Free or Inexpensive Materials," we should send away for them. Every library (or library system) should have a vertical file of these elusive softcover bibliographies. School librarians can use them when the school's curriculum committee is considering introducing a new program. Curriculum committees are notorious for developing courses of study for which no materials exist, and it is an important role of the librarian to let the committee members know in advance what kind of materials support the learning resource center will be able to provide. Public librarians, of course, experience demand for school-related materials, but they also experience demand from the community at large. For instance, a public librarian might have a Girl Scout leader arrive saying, "This year our troop has members whose first language is Spanish. Can you help me find Spanish songs the girls can learn together?" In such a case, the El Paso bibliography would help the librarian to answer the request.

One measure of good professional librarians is that they anticipate demand. They do not look at a specialized list and say, "I'll never need that." They say, "Sooner or later I'm going to need something on that subject so I'd better order it."

New Books

Buying new titles for the collection is one of the real joys of librarianship for most of us. There is a special thrill in opening a box of brand new books and handling each one, deciding which to read first. The question that haunts many beginning librarians is, "What happens if I've made a mistake?" My advice to students who ask this question is to relax. We will all make mistakes throughout our lives. If selection could be made fool-proof, it would mean that all the diversity of human beings would have been eliminated. Expect to make mistakes; just try to learn from them.

If you find that one particular reviewing tool, or reviewer, is consistently misleading you in the selection of certain types of books, stop using the tool for that purpose. At the same time, write a detailed, thoughtful letter to the editor of the periodical explaining your problem. It dismays me to read letters to editors that say, "I didn't like your review of such and such a book and I am canceling my subscription." That is inappropriate behavior for a professional, who should understand that all of us are never going to agree about any given book. (I know people who do not like *Charlotte's Web!*) An antagonistic letter also arouses in the editor or reviewer the urge to defend rather than explain, and defensive responses rarely contribute to genuine communication.

A thoughtful letter, on the other hand, will very likely evoke a thoughtful reply and you may discover that you and the reviewer are operating under different value systems. You will then have to decide whether you should not be happy to have some books in the collection that reflect another point of view. There is also the possibility that yours may not be the first letter on the subject; subsequent investigation by the editorial staff may reveal that the periodical has been trusting the wrong person to do the reviewing.

There are hundreds of sources for reviews of new books, but a librarian who conscientiously works with *Booklist,* the *Bulletin of the Center for Children's Books, Horn Book,* and *School Library Journal* should not miss any important books from the major publishers.

Booklist is an official American Library Association publication; it is published on the first and fifteenth of each month except August, when there is only one issue. *Booklist* has always been a competent reviewing periodical and in recent years has become a superior one. In addition to reviewing adult, young adult, and juvenile books, it now reviews films, filmstrips, video cassettes, multimedia kits, and U.S. Government documents. One important new feature of *Booklist* is its selected bibliographies of foreign children's books. While only the largest libraries will be interested in all the lists, most libraries will find one or more during the course of a year important for providing service to some members of their communities. A major advantage to *Booklist* is that all materials listed are recommended.

Booklist provides numerous cross references among the adult, young adult, and juvenile books being reviewed. A book is reviewed fully in the section where the *Booklist* editors believe it will receive the most use; a much shorter annotation is inserted in other areas where the editors feel it will also have appeal.

Thus, a children's book with young adult appeal will be reviewed in the children's section, with a cross reference inserted in the "Books for Young Adults" section. If the book is basically for young adults but will be useful with older children as well, the review will appear in the young adult section and the referral in the children's.

Booklist also has a special section set aside for "Reference and Subscriptions Books Reviews." This is the only section of *Booklist* that reviews materials that are not recommended. The reviews vary in length from very long to concise (one cannot call any of the reviews short if measured against the length allotted to general trade books). When juvenile encyclopedias are reviewed, I would suggest photocopying the reviews for the professional vertical file, since the question adults most frequently ask children's specialists seems to be, "What encyclopedia should I buy for home use?" I was taught in library school (and subsequently taught other prospective librarians) that one must not offer an opinion but rather provide the materials from which the adult can make a decision. In theory, this is a fine idea and it actually works with some people. I find, however, that when my faculty colleagues from across campus ask me this question, they do not want an exercise in a librarian's objectivity. They want an answer.

I find that I now provide an answer. The decision is based on asking my adult friends a series of questions, beginning, of course, with the number and ages of the children for whom the encyclopedia is intended. In the university setting it is possible to ascertain what kinds of research skills the parents want their children to develop. Learning to use the index in *Compton's* is a different skill from learning to use the cross references in *World Book.* If you develop your own list of questions, you will find that by the time they have been answered, the decision has been made.

Belying its unwieldy title, the *Bulletin of the Center for Children's Books* is easy to use. It has always been a superior book-reviewing tool. Published monthly, except August, by the Graduate Library School of the University of Chicago, it reviews only children's and young adult books and carries no advertising, existing solely on its subscriptions.

The unique feature of the *Bulletin* is its code of symbols, which range from R for Recommended through NR, Not Recommended, to SpR which is the unusual book for the unusual reader. Of particular importance are the Ad and M categories. Ad means that a book is of acceptable quality *if* a library needs more material on this particular subject, but the book has sufficient weaknesses to prevent its being fully recommended. An M book "is so slight in content or has so many weaknesses in style and format that it should be given careful consideration before purchase."

The use of the symbols provides an accurate evaluation of each book considered and leaves space for descriptive comments, thus making the *Bulletin* a most helpful selection source. The symbols also keep us on our toes, alerting us to the fact that we may be buying many Ad books for the collection. This is all right, assuming we actually own the basic books in the category. If we find ourselves buying more than a few M books, we should take time out to assess our standards.

Horn Book, a bimonthly, was the first literary magazine of the children's book world. It is not, and never has been, exclusively geared to the library field and this is its strength. The *Horn Book* is addressed to adults interested in children's literature; its aim is to draw attention to good books, and so it does not usually review books which it does not recommend. All reviewers are identified.

In recent years, *Horn Book* has expanded its coverage to include reviews of phonodiscs, films, and multimedia kits. It has a special section on science books, a section entitled "Of Interest to Adults," and another called "The Hunt Breakfast," which is a potpourri of information about items of interest to both librarians and non-librarians.

The articles in *Horn Book* are an important source of literary analysis. Many are filled with provocative insights into the literary process. Critics, authors, and illustrators write for the magazine and contribute much to our understanding of children's literature.

School Library Journal, issued monthly September through May, has gone through a series of interesting metamorphoses. It began life as "The Children's and Young People's Section" that appeared in every mid-month issue of *Library Journal.* Then it was issued as a separate periodical called *School Library Journal,* while at the same time continuing to appear as part of *LJ.* In January 1975 it became a totally independent publication.

In its early days, *SLJ* had two totally distinct staffs: one for the articles and news content of the magazine, and one for the book review section. This schizophrenic arrangement is now gone; the magazine is totally integrated under one staff and this reorganization has led to improved reviews. With a larger staff, more reviews are written in-house. The outside reviewers are librarians, teachers, and specialists from across the continent. Despite the large number of people reviewing, the periodical now has an evenness of quality that was previously lacking.

SLJ has a review column of professional literature, excellent coverage of the news, and a separate section for letters-to-the-book-review-editor. Annually, it awards its Finn Pin and Budd Button to the worst piece of fiction and the worst picture book of the year. There is a healthy irreverence about *SLJ,* and no school or public librarian should be without it.

Canadian Periodicals

While Canada's major authors, such as Roderick Haig-Brown, Christie Harris, Kay Hill, James Houston, and Farley Mowat are published and reviewed in the United States, there has been a growth of smaller presses within Canada that produce some fine books. Some of these are general presses; others may properly be placed in the "alternative press" category and specialize in feminist books or materials about Native Peoples.

There is much discussion in Canada today about developing a national culture and freeing the country from the overwhelming influence of the United States. As tensions build over the automobile pact and the exportation of Canadian oil and natural gas, it becomes essential that more Americans gain accurate perceptions of the giant to the north. Librarians can promote that understanding by letting children have access to materials written by *Canadians* about Canada. Two periodicals should be in every

Canadian library and available within every school or public library system in the United States.

Canadian Materials, an official publication of the Canadian Library Association, originates in the Canadian School Library Association (CSLA), which provides the editorial board members. It is published three times a year, and its unique feature is that in the Dewey Decimal section of the periodical, all media are integrated, so a book review may be followed by a review of a film, slides, or a filmstrip. It is the only review periodical I know that practices the integration of material that so many of us preach. It is a vital tool for Canadian librarians and important for librarians in other countries who believe in obtaining materials *from* a country rather than limiting the collection to materials *about* a country. All reviews are signed.

In Review: Canadian Books for Children is a quarterly publication of the Ontario Provincial Library. It reviews both English and French children's books and professional materials; offers retrospective reviews of out-of-print books that the editor or the reviewers would like to see reprinted; contains one or more profiles of Canadian authors and illustrators; and usually has at least one article of a general nature. All reviews are signed. It is a superior reviewing periodical and one of the least expensive.

EVALUATING THE SELECTION PROCESS

As stated earlier, we all buy some books we later wish we had not spent money on. When we make a mistake about a piece of clothing or an item for the house, there is always the Salvation Army box to ease our conscience when we decide to toss it out. Some librarians try to ease their conscience about selection mistakes by giving the unwanted books to orphanages, homes for the handicapped, "reform" schools, or other such institutions.

If a book is for some reason not appropriate in a school or public library, both of which have a diverse clientele, why do we think it will be appropriate for children in a special institution? I sympathize with the pain librarians experience when they throw books away, but a mistake is a mistake, and throwing the book away is the only respectable method of correcting the mistake.

The opposite problem—failure to order a good book in the

74

first place—is easier to correct. While the total collection can only be evaluated every five years or so (it takes too much time to go over the whole collection) we can evaluate the previous year's performance fairly easily.

In general terms, we can check our purchases against ALSC's "Notable Children's Books" list and *School Library Journal*'s annual list of the best books of the year. Both school and public librarians should check their holdings against "Classroom Choices," a list of children's trade books for the previous year that appears in the *Reading Teacher* in its November issue. This list is a joint effort of members of the International Reading Association and the Children's Book Council. Books on this list have actually been used with children. Inclusion does not represent hypothetical judgments by adults but actual responses of children.

In the social studies area, *Social Education*, the periodical of the National Council for the Social Studies, in cooperation with the Children's Book Council, publishes an annual list, "Notable Children's Trade Books in the Field of Social Studies," in its December issue. If you find that you do not own most of the books on the list, you may have discovered a weakness in the selection tools you are using or a weakness in your priorities.

The same statement can be made if you do not own most of the books appearing on the annual "Outstanding Science Trade Books for Children in [year]" which appears in the March issue of *Science and Children*. This is, again, a cooperative effort—between the National Science Teachers Association and the Children's Book Council.

It is interesting that the lists produced by the non-library groups always spell out in precise terms the criteria used to select the books and that they identify the person who wrote the annotation. It would be a step forward if official lists from divisions of ALA adopted a similar procedure.

AUDIOVISUAL MATERIALS

Audiovisual materials are essential, but their selection is time-consuming. First, potentially useful materials must be identified from reviews; then they must be requested for previewing; then they must be previewed; finally, they must be purchased or returned to the vendor.

There are some independent libraries wealthy enough to build their own film collection, but most school and public libraries must be part of a larger, centralized system to have access to a wide range of films. Whether that system is a school system or a cooperative public library system, the selection procedures are similar: a professional librarian orders materials for previewing and a previewing committee views or listens to materials and votes the final decision.

While all school and public library systems should have large back-up collections, each local unit should have its own collection of slides, filmstrips, cassettes, and phonodiscs. The collection should reflect the priorities each librarian has established (see Chapter 1).

Selection of audiovisual materials must be based on knowledge. To gain that knowledge, I would recommend regular reading of *Media & Methods* and *Previews*.

Media & Methods is the most exciting periodical that comes across my desk. It is concerned with the total educational process and presents an integrated media approach to the subject. There are articles on such subjects as censorship and how to recognize your value-prejudices, as well as philosophical interviews with people like Jonathan Kozol. There is practical information on such topics as using old-time radio program tapes in the school and producing your own materials. All this plus reviews, opinions, and informative advertising.

Previews is the Bowker audiovisual counterpart to *Library Journal* and *School Library Journal* and is limited to coverage of non-book materials so as not to compete with *Lj* and *SLj*. Its reviews are divided by type of material, *e.g.*, 16mm films, prints, spoken-word recordings, etc. Within each category, the material covered is arranged alphabetically by subject rather than by the more traditional Dewey Decimal system. *Previews* contains news and views, articles, and mediagraphic essays on specific subjects, as well as special listings such as the previous year's best popular records.

76

Library systems that are serious about their film collections should be members of the Educational Film Library Association (EFLA) and send at least one staff person to EFLA's annual Festival of Films. The festival runs for a week and participants can view the films that are in contention for the Blue and Red Ribbon awards—films that have been screened by many committees throughout the year. The festival ends with an all day showing of the prize films in each category.

EFLA members can arrange to be on the circuit of the Blue and Red Ribbon winners and hold their own local film festivals. Since the films cut across all age limits, sponsoring a local film festival is an excellent opportunity for the children's, young adult, and adult services librarians to work together and to encourage library programming that is not geared to one specific age group.

THE ALTERNATIVE PRESS

Keeping track of what is being issued by the major publishing houses is no problem. Keeping track of books from the smaller, geographically dispersed alternative presses is much more difficult. Most of us are spoiled. We want to have books brought to our attention, not to have to go hunting for them; but if we are to buy small-press products, we have to learn to browse in bookstores that carry such titles.

Booklegger ° and *Emergency Librarian* are essential periodicals for keeping informed about small-press offerings. Both run regular review columns and both periodically devote a major portion of an issue to children's library services.

While the major national chains of bookstores have not been enthusiastic about stocking titles from small presses, all feminist and gay bookstores have been very good about offering their patrons a wide selection of alternative-press books. Independent bookstores in smaller cities and towns have also begun to stock these elusive materials, discovering that they have a steady clientele for the books.

The problem many librarians face is the bureaucratic red tape

° As this book went to press, *Booklegger* was in a temporary state of discontinuance.

involved in purchasing materials. Some communities require that the treasurer or town manager sign all purchase orders; some require that all purchase orders be put out to bid. We all understand that these procedures have been developed to guarantee that tax monies are spent fairly and wisely. But when procedures keep us from being able to walk into a bookstore and buy needed materials for our libraries, or keep us from placing direct mail orders with small presses, then we have to work to change the procedures.

Since change takes time, a temporary solution to this problem is to have the Parent-Teacher Association (Home-School Association in Canada) or the public library's Friends of the Library group provide a fund that can be used at the discretion of the librarian. The people who belong to such organizations are concerned about library service or the overall quality of the school program, and they can be very effective allies in helping us explain that traditional puchasing procedures are not appropriate to all situations.

New librarians, or older librarians who have been ignoring the small presses, should study *Alternatives in Print*, compiled regularly by the SRRT Task Force on AIP. *Alternatives in Print* is a multi-media bibliography, despite its name, so it provides us with access to all types of materials in the United States and Canada, as well as in Europe.

The importance of buying small-press publications is a measure of our commitment to providing the widest range of attitudes possible in the children's collection. As observed in Chapter 2, the traditional publishers provide us with a very narrow range of attitudes. The small-press books may not be of the production quality we are used to accepting, but viewpoints expressed more than make up for defects in production techniques.

PART TWO:

Library Services

CHAPTER
SIX

The Child in the Library

EVERY LIBRARY needs some rules and regulations, not only to govern the use of its facilities and collection but also to promote such use by its patrons. The number and nature of those regulations will distinguish those libraries that welcome children from those that wish children would disappear from the scene.

Rules exist primarily to assure equal treatment for all library users and only secondarily to make the running of the library as easy as possible for the librarian. Therefore, each rule formulated should be considered first in relationship to its effect on the borrower and only then in relationship to the convenience of the library staff. In the long run, rules made because they seem the easiest way out of a difficult situation often prove extremely troublesome. For example, public libraries experiencing problems with crowds of children and adolescents in the evening sometimes yield to the temptation to impose a ban on non-adult borrowers during those hours. Such a ban tells the perceptive observer that the librarians in question care little about providing service to youth. Rules ought to reflect a library's philosophy of service. When the rules are in conflict with *stated* policies of service, members of the community are within their rights in demanding that the school or library board restate the policies or change the rules.

USE OF THE LIBRARY

Use of the public library is the right of every citizen, regardless of age. It is not a privilege to be bestowed or withheld by the librarians or the board of trustees. Indeed, the librarian as chief administrator has the responsibility to make membership in the library as simple as possible.

In recent years this view has been challenged, most notably in the report of the New York State Commissioner of Education's Committee on the Development of Library Services,[1] which recommended that all library service to children be offered through school libraries. While the financial restraints of the past few years has kept this recommendation from being tested in pilot projects, it is not a dead issue and will periodically surface.

Aside from all the questions that come to mind about the practicality of implementing such a recommendation (see Burke and Shields, *Children's Library Service*[2]), there is the basic question of the rights of children. ALA's Library Bill of Rights states that use of the library should not be abridged because of age. A public library refusing to serve children would find itself in conflict with that principle, and while the Library Bill of Rights is often subtly or overtly ignored by many librarians, it is highly unlikely that many librarians would be willing to stand up in their communities and say that the Library Bill of Rights was hogwash. It is equally unlikely that the ALA Council could be convinced to rewrite the document to eliminate the word *age*. The argument that would carry the day in Council is that once the profession agreed to curtail access to libraries for one segment of the population, it would open the gates to curtailment of use for other groups.

Children already have major limitations imposed upon them in their search for library materials to meet their needs. Theodore Hines has pointed out that "such networking as does exist exists for grownups."[3] Many libraries will not interloan children's materials. Despite all the discussions of individualized learning and all the lip service paid to the idea that every human has his or her own developmental pattern, the fact remains that too many adults—teachers, parents, and librarians—would really be happiest if all children could be forced into a homogeneous group. That would limit the demands made upon adults working or living with them.

The "duplication" of materials in school and public libraries that concerns some surveyors is not a genuine issue. It would disappear if school and public libraries embarked on a sound interlibrary loan policy, because once such a policy was instituted and enthusiastically supported by librarians, data would soon reveal that children need more, not fewer, points of access to the sources of information. This is particularly true in relationship to non-book resources.

Rather than discuss how to limit children's use of the public library, I believe we should be talking about how to eliminate some of the regulations that presently impose restrictions on use. The first of these is insistence on parental signatures to obtain a library card. If the library accepts the interpretation of the Library Bill of Rights that says librarians should not act *in loco parentis* when it comes to lending materials, then the library should also grant library cards to the children who request them and leave it up to the parents to tell their children not to use the library.

Before developing the reasons that lead me to believe that all children should be issued library cards on request, it is necessary to point out that the small word *if* that occurs in the preceding paragraph is of monumental importance. There is a disturbing increase in the number of news items reporting that library systems in the United States have developed forms that parents can fill out on which they specify books they do not want their children to borrow. The library staff then assumes responsibility for enforcing these restrictions. This procedure means that the library staff must check a file of some sort for each child borrowing materials to see if parental restrictions have been instituted.

A variation on this procedure is to code children's cards so that those bearing a particular symbol are barred from borrowing any adult materials. In both cases, the library has assumed the role of mediator between parents and their children. A more appropriate position for the library to take would hold that conflicts between parents and children are not the concern of an institution whose goal is the provision of information for all who want it.

When I have raised the point of issuing library cards without parental consent in verbal discussions with librarians, most respond by thinking up objections. I have heard them all. "It won't work" is the typical response, no reasons given for the opinion. More subtly, someone will say, "Do you mean that we just issue cards to four-year-olds if they want them?" Yes, that is precisely what I mean.

Under what circumstances are we apt to encounter four-year-olds in a public library? They can have come with one or both parents, in which case we can operate under the principle of implied consent. They can come with an older sibling, in which case we can assume that they are as likely to return as is the sister or brother they are with, so they represent no greater potential delinquency. Or perhaps they come as part of a group from a nearby daycare center or nursery school, in which case we know they will be returning with the group on its next visit.

Why should we offer four-year-olds cards on their own recognizance? Primarily because the only way to learn to be responsible is to be held responsible for one's own actions. For many children, possession of their own library card is a great moment in their young lives. It may be the first time that young children are given a glimpse of the fact that they are individuals and not appendages to their parents. If we add to this the fact that getting a library card may be the first independent action children take, we can see that they may carry a positive image of the library with them throughout life. And certainly, libraries could do with more people growing to adulthood thinking of them in positive, friendly terms.

Most school librarians assume that any child attending school is entitled to use the library, although there are some few who still impose restrictions, such as demonstrated ability to read. School librarians are more likely to curtail children's use of the library by limiting the time of day or times during the week when they can use the library. It is interesting to note that school librarians in general do not require parental signatures for issuing library cards. I made this observation to some public librarians and the response was, "But the school librarian can assume parents want their children to use all the school facilities." Not true, say I, or why do schools constantly send home forms for

84

permission to go on a field trip, participate in sports, or other activities?

Some school systems have moved beyond this point and now require parental permission for a child to take the family life program; some school systems have moved to the point of granting parents the right to object to the use of a particular textbook or to object to assigned outside (e.g., non-textbook) reading. All of these actions are curtailments of the rights of children and sooner or later all of us are going to have to face squarely the question of whether children have the right to learn what they want to learn or are limited by their parents' views of what is acceptable knowledge. In my opinion, it would be inappropriate for librarians to formulate any regulations that restrict the rights of children.

Registration Procedures

One attitude that school and public librarians seem to share is the viewing of the registration procedure as something to be gotten over with in the speediest way possible. Nothing seems to please them more than to register an entire class at one time. From the librarians' point of view, registration is a clerical procedure, and the reluctance to spend a lot of time on it is understandable. But from the children's point of view, this is an important event. If it is necessary to do mass registrations, the librarian should stress to the children that the first time they come to the library on their own, they should ask for their own private introduction to the library and its services.

When children register for cards in a public library, they should be introduced to the entire library, but detailed descriptions of the portions they are most likely to be using should be stressed. This need not be a lengthy procedure, and certainly should not take the form of a lecture, but rather as a sharing of information with the purpose of helping children know what they can expect from the library and conveying to them what we expect of them. Children do appreciate this knowledge; it helps them feel secure and comfortable in the library. It also impresses upon them that this is a mutual undertaking in which both par-

85

ties—the patron and the library—have rights and responsibilities.

One of the basic questions to be resolved in formulating borrowing procedures is that of how many books, records, filmstrips, or other materials may be borrowed by a patron at one time and how long these materials may be kept. Also, can the materials be renewed? And if so, for how long, and under what circumstances? Will the library reserve books for children? (If it does so for adults, the answer should be yes.) If we operate on the assumption that restrictions should never be imposed unless absolutely necessary, our regulations will be fair and impose no hardship on the patrons.

Another attitude that school librarians and public librarians have in common is the acceptance of a hierarchy of users, with the children, for whom, supposedly, the collection exists, being at the lowest end of the list. Certainly there are times when we extend special rights to persons with special needs—e.g., someone doing a master's thesis on children's literature—and that is perfectly acceptable as long as we can also recognize the special needs of children and are prepared to offer them similar prerogatives.

ACCESSIBILITY

Access to the collection comes in two forms: internal and external. *Internal accessibility* means that children are free to use the entire library. *External accessibility* involves analysis of the transportation patterns of the community, the hours of the school day, and the location of the building to insure that people can get to the library at times convenient to them.

Library hours should be determined by the behavior patterns of the potential users and not by the convenience of the librarians. This may sound so reasonable as to not be worth stating, but the following is a true story. One metropolitan library system in the midwest announced that a particular branch library would close at 8:30 p.m. instead of 9:00 p.m. in order to allow the librarian to catch a bus. At least the library was honest about its motivations and its value system, but that is all that can be said for that type of decision-making.

It is important to remember that each community has its own

patterns of behavior and the library should fit itself into those patterns, not try to change them or exist outside of them. Community patterns can and do change—creation of a new shopping center, construction of a new highway—and librarians must reevaluate the situation each time one of these events occurs. For children's librarians, school construction or relocation is vital information that may affect the use of the library by children.

Remember, there is little sense in offering internal accessibility to children if they cannot use the library because of external factors. We cannot control the externals, so it is essential that we know what they are and adapt ourselves to them.

DISCIPLINE

No problem has gone through as many stages of examination as that of discipline within the library. I began in the era when silence was the rule; we moved from that to "the busy hum" position. (The busy hum was supposed to be a sign that the children were working together in the spirit of teamwork advocated by the newest educational theory.) In the late 1960s and early 1970s, school libraries began to be built that provided facilities for both group work and individualized learning. Some, but not many, sections in public libraries exist where children can listen to a phonodisc or a cassette, but the full range of audiovisual equipment and materials found in so many school libraries is sadly lacking in most public library facilities.

The physical conditions within a library have as much to do with whether there is control or chaos as does the attitude the library staff brings to the question. If a public library allots the smallest amount of space to the largest group of users, forcing them to knock into each other, trip over each other, and sit at large tables, then it has only itself to blame when the noise level rises and conflicts occur between the children.

One of the interesting findings from the study of body language is that some people need more space than others. (Space, in this sense, is defined as the distance between two people that allows them to feel comfortable and unthreatened.) Researchers

87

have found that men in prison for physical assault need more space in order to feel unthreatened than most of the population. [4] Among children, physical closeness inspires aggression in some and not in others. It may be that the children we find ourselves labeling as troublemakers simply need more space; it is at least worth thinking about, because it is very hard to justify penalizing people simply because they have different space needs than most of us. On the other hand, if we keep this difference in mind, we just may be able to resolve a problem with particular children by providing them with more space without making them feel they are being excluded.

The attitude of the library staff is vital in establishing the atmosphere within the library. Some librarians encounter no—or few—discipline problems even under the most horrendous physical conditions. Others, working in almost ideal quarters, are besieged by problems. In all but the most exceptional circumstances, persistent discipline problems can be traced to poor attitudes by the staff toward children. Too often staff see their role as *controlling* children rather than as creating an atmosphere that encourages self-discipline. "Self-discipline" is one of those tautologies that has crept into our language. Discipline *is* self-imposed. Control is imposed by others.

Attempts to control other people, from the youngest to the oldest, inspire rebellion in all but the most docile. If we create the conditions that inspire rebellion, we have only ourselves to blame when it occurs.·

What are the conditions that indicate we are striving for control? First is a demonstrated lack of respect for children. In *Escape from Childhood,* John Holt wrote of the parents who told him "that most of the time they tried to behave toward their then four-year-old son as if he were a very distinguished visitor from a strange and alien civilization, knowing little but eager to learn about how we do things here." [5] It is a fine analogy and one worth incorporating into our view of children. It is almost impossible for most of us to be disrespectful to people who show respect for us, and that is as true of children as for adults.

One of the ways in which we demonstrate disrespect for children is by having triple standards—one for them, one for adults using the library, and one for the library staff. I have attended meetings of librarians devoted to discussing the uproar young people create in libraries and then seen us create more noise leaving the meeting room than any group of children ever did. Yet we did not feel our natural exuberance and enjoyment of being with each other was an assault upon the order of the library hosting us. We were not maliciously disrupting the library or deliberately annoying its patrons—but whatever our motivation, we were doing both. Where too many of us go astray in dealing with children is that *we attribute to them malicious intent.* Once we come to believe that they are deliberately misbehaving, it becomes easy to go the next step and order, "Get out!" Such behavior on our part serves to declare war.

While Haim Ginott's *Between Parent and Child*[6] may be too simplified a presentation for clinical psychologists, it has much to tell us about how to relate to children without making them feel worthless. There is no real difference between a parent's response to spilt milk and the librarian's response to a child knocking over a plant or a display. To make children feel inadequate as human beings because of a clumsy action is a terrible thing to do to them.

Once we have established for ourselves just what are our attitudes toward children within the library and what kind of behavior is acceptable, we must share this information by posting it on a bulletin board and otherwise making our expectations known, perhaps as part of a brochure that explains the rules of the library and the resources available. We can explain to children that the information in the brochure represents a contract: The library offers these services and in exchange requires this level of behavior from its patrons.

It is then necessary that we as librarians be as consistent as possible in living up to the contract. It is inevitable that we will all have bad days when a noise level ordinarily acceptable becomes unbearable. The best way to handle this situation is to be honest with the children and tell them we are in a rotten mood. They understand this since they go through it at home. All children learn to "cool it" when a parent is in a bad mood. They recognize similar moods in teachers; it will not ruin our relationship with them to share the knowledge that librarians are also human.

89

The worst way to handle a problem is to blow up. Acting childishly is inappropriate per se, but it also will make the children very uncertain about what to expect from us. Furthermore, it may arouse in them the temptation to see how much madder they can make us.

There will always be occasions when we have to play a police role and throw someone out. If we tell a child, "Next time I have to speak to you, out you go," we must be sure we mean it and will follow through. We must not keep threatening and never acting on the threat. That technique simply challenges the child to see how far we can be pushed.

Finally, it is absolutely necessary to explain to children why we are objecting to their behavior. The more specific we can be, the better off we are. Telling children that they are "too noisy" indicates that there is a level of noise that is acceptable, and we should be able to define the line that separates the two.

How children respond to our invoking authority depends on the community we are serving. Some librarians work in communities where the children are taught to respond docilely to orders from non-parental adults. They will go meekly, when ordered out. Some children will go defiantly, but they will go. Some communities, however, give their children the idea that the world belongs to them and they can do as they please. In the last-named situation, a child is apt to respond, "You can't throw me out. This is a public library and my parents pay taxes." If we respond, "I can too. I'm boss around here," we are, in the words of transactional analysis,[7] responding from our "Parent." The "Adult" response is to point out objectively that the library exists to serve all patrons and its rules must be obeyed the same ways rules of the road are. Breaking them results in paying a penalty.

The nature of the penalty should also be specific. We can say that the child may return in thirty minutes if he or she thinks that is enough time to decide to behave. We can say, "That's it for today. Try again tomorrow." But we should not ban children for longer than overnight. Imposing a week's ban, for example, is out of line with the offense.

In all this, we are talking about ordinary children, guilty of nothing more than exuberance carried a step too far. Children who physically assault other children or who engage in genuine antisocial behavior require help. Public librarians still too rarely involve themselves with these children, but they should. They can use the same resources available to a school librarian: talking to the child's teachers, consulting the school psychologist, etc. In fact one of the most important reasons for a public librarian to have good communication lines with the school librarian is to find out whether the child's behavior in the library is unique or usual.

How we handle the question of establishing and maintaining discipline in the library depends upon the kind of people we are. Some of us prefer the light touch; some of us are very formal. Both methods work well as long as they are consistent with our personalities. What does not work is heavy-handed authoritarian behavior. If we find ourselves thinking always in terms of being boss, using terms like *my library,* we are in for trouble. People who need to feel "in charge" all the time are usually frightened of losing control over a situation. While it strikes me as strange that people who are basically afraid of children would choose to work with them, it does happen. Children instinctively sense that fear, they know that fear means insecurity, and they are quick to take advantage of it.

If we have a constant trouble with discipline, the problem no doubt lies more with us than with the children. A periodic review of the three basic rules in relating to children—a single standard of behavior for all, meaning what we say, and adequate explanations of our objections—will probably reveal a failure on our part in practicing one or more of them. If we have trouble analyzing our own behavior, we can ask someone else on the staff to be an objective observer, or better yet, if the library owns video equipment, we can have a day in the library filmed and see our behavior as captured by the camera. It can be a chastening experience, but worth the momentary pain if it leads to improved behavior.

FLOOR WORK WITH CHILDREN

Children, like all other library patrons, arrive at the library with diverse needs. Much of the writing in the children's field leads us to conclude that most children arrive wanting our advice about a good book to read. Some children do, but they are in a minority, and we rarely find ourselves giving reader's advisory service until after we have established a personal relationship with the individual child.

Elementary school librarians and children's librarians in public libraries are more apt to find themselves giving reader's advisory service to adults than to children. School librarians are called upon to create bibliographies for units being taught; public librarians are often asked for advice about appropriate books for a sick child. Or a concerned teacher or parent will be looking for books to motivate a particular child to read and will ask our help. Only a minority of the children ask for reader's advisory service. If we are to offer advisory service to children, *we* must create the circumstances, not wait for them to demand it.

Reference service, on the other hand, is a very important part of library work with children. In fact, to be a good children's librarian we must have the skills of a good reference librarian. Reference skills fall into two categories: personal characteristics and professional knowledge.

Personal Characteristics

A good librarian must exude *receptivity,* making it easy for children to approach the desk and ask their questions. If the reference desk is out on the floor, the chances are that library policy requires the librarian to be "doing something" while assigned there. Book reviews are read, materials are selected for the vertical file, and internal memos are read and/or written. The task being done is not important. What is important is that a good librarian develops peripheral vision so that children wandering around, too frightened to interrupt the librarian, are spotted quickly. Good librarians know where everyone is at any given moment.

Mobility is important. Besides looking up, we should get up from the chair and take a walk around the room at regular intervals. Even if no one needs any help, it does not hurt to pause and ask, "Are you finding what you want?" Even when the answer to that question is, "Yes, thank you," we have made the point that we are willing to help.

Friendliness and *sensitivity* are vital characteristics. We do not have to become "buddies" with the children, but we must display enough good humor to make it clear that we do not consider their questions an intrusion. Sensitivity is needed to understand the shy child's reluctance to ask for help.

Professional Characteristics

Whether we are being asked for a good book to read or the design for an Iroquois longhouse, we must see questions as challenges and not impositions. When questions are for school work or a Brownie assignment, it is hard to keep in mind that even though the question has been asked of us by a dozen previous children, it is still brand new to the child asking it now. Good librarians learn to resist the temptation to become irritable under such circumstances.

Irritability, a harsh answer, or sarcasm are sure to defeat our purposes. Children treated to these responses will think twice about asking for help again.

Every librarian knows that few patrons, children or adults, ask for what they actually want. A good librarian takes the time to establish the specific nature of the patron's needs. For example, the child who actually wants a design of an Iroquois longhouse may begin by asking for books about Native People, or for a book on houses. Learning to ascertain the specific nature of a question without turning the session into a third-degree interrogation is one of the most highly valued skills in a reference librarian. It is a skill that comes with time; few of us are born with it.

Perhaps the biggest mistake for experienced librarians is jumping to conclusions. If we have been at one library for a period of time, we begin to know the cycles of school or Scout assignments. We know almost to the day when the third grade will begin its project on Native People, and if someone arrives with a question on that topic, we tend to automatically hear it as part of the school assignment. We should remember that every question that is asked for a school assignment can also be asked by someone who simply wants to know the answer for personal reasons, and the same answer may not serve both needs.

Finally, a good reference librarian uses all the resources of the library. If someone asks about Christmas customs in Mexico and all the books on Mexico are in circulation, we may remember that picture books like *Nine Days to Christmas*, by Marie Hall Ets and Aurora Labastida, may tell enough to satisfy the patron's needs. Similarly, Alice Goudey's *Houses from the Sea* may be precisely what the child needs in order to find out about seashells. Lancelot Hogben's *The Wonderful World of Mathematics* offers an excellent description of how the Egyptian pyramids were built. Thorough knowledge of the library's collection will cut to a minimum the number of unanswered questions.

Many adult books are also of importance in answering children's questions. But even more important are adult magazines. If a Scout troop is planning a weekend hiking trip and is looking for easy-to-prepare recipes, the adult magazines on camping and trailering are excellent sources for menus.

It is not necessary to read every issue of every magazine the library subscribes to, but all librarians should browse through four or five issues of each magazine to understand its scope and become familiar with its special features. In many cases, the most valuable information for reference service will not be indexed in *Readers' Guide to Periodical Literature,* and only our own knowledge will unlock it when we need it.

Reader's Advisory Service

The term reader's advisory service can mean the simple act of finding a child a book for a book report. Or it can mean introducing children to books they might never find on their own without our help. The former is a specific response to a child's request; the latter involves a generalized attitude that should permeate our work.

Displays should always contain at least one or two titles for the more sophisticated reader. It would not be inappropriate to put Mari Sandoz's *The Horsecatcher* with a display of run-of-the-mill horse stories, for example.

Displays can also serve to broaden children's concepts of the world. Too often displays or booklists about Native People are limited to the United States' boundaries, yet there are Native People in Central and South America as well as in Canada. A large map of the two continents as a backdrop enables us to present Native People in a way that helps children understand that there is more to the issue of Native rights than the views presented on television reruns of old westerns.

However we approach the question of how to broaden our patrons' viewpoint, we should understand that every display we set up, every booklist we create, is a statement of our value system. If everything we do is innocuous, neutral, that tells us that we are opting for the status quo. If we take chances, recommend books that are potentially troublesome, we have opted for educating our patrons.

The books we stand up on top of the bookcases are political statements. Why this one and not that one?

It is essential that all of us think through what it is we are trying to accomplish and act accordingly. While I am unhappy with librarians who operate in neutral gear, I am even more unhappy with librarians who provoke trouble without any philosophical premise behind their actions. I believe, for example, that at least once a year every library should have a display of books on sex and sexuality. But if the librarian is not truly convinced that children have a right to think, read, and talk about sex—only that such a display would be exciting—then trouble can be the only result.

95

NOTES FOR CHAPTER 6

1. "A Statement of Policy and Proposed Action by the Regents of the University of the State of New York," Albany: The State Education Department, October 1970. Reprinted in Burke and Shields (see footnote 2).
2. J. Gordon Burke, and Gerald R. Shields, *Children's Library Service*, Metuchen, NJ: Scarecrow Press, 1974.
3. Theodore Hines, "Children's Access to Libraries," in Zena Sutherland, and May Hill Arbuthnot, *Children and Books*, 5th ed., Glenview, IL: Scott Foresman, 1977, pp. 624-7.
4. Julius Fast, *Body Language*, New York: Pocket Bks, 1970.
5. John Holt, *Escape from Childhood; The Needs and Rights of Childhood*, New York: Ballantine Bks, 1975, p. 217.
6. Haim Ginott, *Between Parent and Child*, New York: Avon Bks, 1969.
7. Thomas Harris, *I'm OK—You're OK*, New York: Avon Bks, 1973.

CHAPTER
SEVEN

Programs for Children

LIBRARY PROGRAMS for children are not frills; on the contrary, they constitute a basic ingredient in a carefully thought-out plan of service. Programs serve a number of purposes: they enrich the background and stimulate the interest of the children who are already library patrons; they can bring into the library children who do not ordinarily use its services; and, finally, they can provide librarians with direct feedback as to the interests of the children.

There is more creative programming being done today than ever before; only staff, time, and money limit what librarians can do. The most important quideline in setting up a program schedule is to remember it is better to do four programs a year and do them well than to do one a week in a slipshod manner. It is not the quantity but the quality that is important.

PRESCHOOL PROGRAMS

In many ways, the preschool program for the three- and four-year-olds is both the hardest and easiest to execute. It is the hardest because it requires the most careful planning on the part of the librarian; because it requires the librarian to have a sound knowledge of the characteristics of young children; and because it involves both the children and their parents. It is the easiest because preschoolers are the most enthusiastic group of children to work with.

No less important than the knowledge of what a preschool program should be is the recognition on the part of parents of what it should not be. It is not a free baby-sitting service designed to give parents an hour to shop. Nor is it a substitute for nursery school or a daycare center. When properly planned and executed, the program is an introduction to good books and to being a member of a group, and constitutes the first lesson in group listening. The child who is not ready for these experiences has to be excluded from the group, however awkward this may be for the librarian.

Since young children are easily distracted, it is unwise to plan a preschool program unless there is a separate room available, or a nook removed from the main stream of traffic. And since the parents or other adults who bring the children to the program should be required to remain in the building, there should be additional space for adults to be comfortable. Some librarians have been successful in scheduling adult discussion groups at the same time as the preschool program. This is one solution to the problem of keeping the adults happy within the building without making them feel as if they are imprisoned. However, many may welcome the opportunity to browse or talk with other adults and will be happier on their own.

It cannot be stressed too strongly that there must be one responsible adult in the building for each child attending the preschool program. Young children placed in a group of strangers are frightened, regardless of the bravado they may display. And if one child in the group panics, the others are apt to follow suit. Children also can become ill or need to go the toilet. The librarian conducting the program cannot leave the group unattended without chaos resulting, so the need for adults to be within range is vital.

The program, often referred to as preschool hour, must be planned carefully, and each week should see a small increase in the length of time the children are asked to sit and the maturity of the story read to them. In the beginning, twenty minutes is as long as we should expect young children to remain attentive. The librarian can extend this period of time by leading the children in stand-in-place exercises between stories.

There are certain standards of behavior we should expect from the children if the program is to achieve its aims. They must listen to the story without interrupting, although they can be expected to chime in if the story has a repetitive phrase, such as, "hundreds of cats, thousands of cats, millions and billions and trillions of cats." If use of *Curious George Rides a Bike* provokes from a child the comment, "I have a bike," the librarian simply nods to acknowledge having heard the comment but does not stop to discuss the size and color of the child's bike. It is appropriate at the end of the story to talk with the children about bicycles or cats or whatever the topic, but while the story is being read, the children should be expected to sit quietly and listen. Total silence is never the goal, but a semblance of order is.

In a preschool program the librarian also has a responsibility to read the book as written. We do not stop along the way to ask questions or to deliver small lectures or explanations. I have seen librarians ruin *Make Way for Ducklings* by stopping at the point where the mother duck leads her ducklings across the street and delivering a lecture on why we should never cross streets without police supervision or a traffic light to aid us. I have seen librarians interrupt *The Story About Ping* to point out that the little duck would not have had all those troubles if he had been willing to accept the punishment for being the last to return to the boat. There is no excuse for librarians delivering such minilectures. The lessons may be important but they are not part of the librarian's responsibility during a preschool program.

Children who continually interrupt the story or wander around the room or poke at their neighbors are not ready for a group program, and if, after a warning or two, they do not respond, they should be asked to leave. A certain amount of restlessness is to be expected, but good planning will keep it to a minimum.

The film *The Pleasure Is Mutual*[1] shows the many and varied ways in which experienced librarians conduct preschool programs. It is an excellent training film and should be viewed by in-service trainees before they are faced with the actual situation.

While some very experienced librarians can deal with hordes

of young children, most of us should plan for a maximum of twenty children at preschool programs. Because of colds, measles, and other childhood ailments, the actual group will usually number between fifteen and eighteen each week. It is a good idea to require parents to register their children, making the program appear a little more formal, and thus to be taken a little more seriously, than might otherwise be the case. By this technique, we accomplish two important aims: children are made more secure by seeing the same faces each week, and the librarian is not forced to cope with forty children one week and six the next.

When the number of potential participants far exceeds the number that can be easily accommodated, the first twenty children should be scheduled for a session for six to eight weeks, then the next twenty scheduled for a similar length of time, and so on, until all the children wanting to attend have been given the experience. Rotating the groups is a far better solution than trying to do a preschool program for fifty or more children. It is vital to keep the size of the audience down, not to make life easier on ourselves, but because the pictures in the book being read must be seen by every child in the room. When the group is too large, it is impossible to seat the children so they can all see and this creates unrest.

If we find that we have a large waiting list for future preschool programs, it is good public relations to schedule preschool films or puppet shows at least once each month. Films and puppet shows can be seen by much larger numbers of children than the traditional picture book. By providing something of interest for those children who cannot be accommodated in the preschool program, we tell the community that the library cares about all children. The librarian also has an opportunity to explain to parents the necessity for small groups when dealing with books without creating ill will by excluding their children entirely from the library's programming.

With an increase in nursery schools and daycare centers, many librarians find themselves scheduling visits for these groups just as they have always scheduled visits from school classes. If there are nursery schools or daycare centers within the boundaries

100

served by the library, special invitations should be extended for these groups to visit. The format for dealing with such groups is exactly the same as that for dealing with the library's preschool program, except that the librarian should briefly show the children around the library the first time the group visits.

To a librarian, one of the most satisfying groups of young visitors is a class of mentally or physically handicapped children. Too many of us do not firmly believe that handicapped children can benefit from the library. Yet, as every librarian who has had the experience can testify, these children are fun to tell stories to and to show around the library.

PICTURE BOOK PROGRAMS

The picture book program is often confused with the preschool program. This confusion arises because both rely heavily on the use of the picture book for program material. There, however, the similarity ends.

The picture book program is for school-age children from five to seven—roughly kindergarten through second grade. This group has more self-assurance than the preschool group, but lacks sufficient maturity for the story hour. These children will listen better, sit longer, and enjoy more mature and complicated stories than preschoolers. They are also ready for the simple folk or fairy tale told without using a book. This is the beginning of the child's ability to visualize the way the characters look and how the events take place without having to accept the illustrator's ideas.

Children in the picture book group need special attention for two important reasons. First, they are at the stage of beginning to read themselves and all too often, unfortunately, this has marked the end of their being read to at home. Withdrawal of the time spent on a parent's lap or being read to before the light is put out at bedtime, can lead some children to refuse to learn to read. Some children develop real reading problems at school because they are subconsciously rebelling against learning to read—they believe it deprives them of being read to at home. While the library's picture book program cannot replace that

101

home warmth, it can show children that we care. It can also help motivate them to learn to read by reminding them that books contain all those wonderful, funny, exciting stories.

The second reason for providing children of this age with their own programs is that we can then exclude them from the older story hour group without feeling guilty. If we do not exclude them, the story hour tends to become a picture book program and the older children lose interest. While some programs can appeal to a wide age range, the story hour should be reserved for older children.

THE STORY HOUR

Many librarians report that the story hour, designed for children from third grade up, is no longer worth doing because of low attendance. This is unfortunate, since the story hour is the opportunity to introduce children to some of the great stories, myths, and legends of human history.

The popularity of the story hour varies from community to community. If the library serves a middle-class, suburban community where the children are expected to take dancing and tennis lessons, go to the Y weekly, attend Scouts and innumerable other socializing activities, then there probably will be few children available for, or interested in, a library story hour.

If the children in the area served by the library are not over-programmed but story hour attendance is still falling off, then the librarian should look to see what is wrong with the story hours being offered. Perhaps young children have been allowed to attend, and their restlessness and chatter have driven the older ones away. Perhaps the librarian has begun to gear the selection of stories to this young group. Perhaps the librarian really doesn't enjoy telling stories and it shows. There is also the possibility that the story hours are scheduled at inappropriate times.

Holding a story hour is not mandatory, and if your situation indicates that other types of programs will be more successful, then do them and do not feel guilty about not having a story hour. Many of the values of a story hour can be built into other programs, most notably puppet shows, which will be discussed below.

Librarians who want to try story hours should study the film *There's Something About a Story*[2] for techniques. There are a number of books about storytelling (see bibliography), but it is important to remember there is a big difference between being a professional storyteller and being a librarian who tells stories as one small part of the job. If we like the stories we tell and know them well enough to tell without stumbling and mumbling, the children will enjoy them.

Both school and public librarians have occasions when they have a captive audience; a class visit to the library offers an excellent opportunity to tell a story. It is a good idea to collect stories that can be told in five minutes or less and to put the basic plot line of each on a three-by-five card so that we can refresh our memory of the story even if the book containing it is in circulation.

Storytelling is a rewarding activity and it serves to introduce children to many of the books in the folk and fairy tale section of the library. If we select mature enough stories to tell, we can break down the idea that fairy tales are for "little children." Actually, folk and fairy tales are enjoyed most by children in the fourth, fifth, and sixth grades once they can overcome the idea that such reading material is beneath them.

PUPPET SHOWS

Puppet shows have become an important element in library programming. They can be as simple or complex in their production as the skills and talents of the staff make possible. In common with film programs, they appeal to a wide age range, including adults.

If we do not personally possess the skills to make puppets, it is possible to recruit students from a high school arts-and-crafts course to make the puppets. We can also recruit members of the high school drama club to write and perform the scripts. The woodworking class can build the stage and other necessary props. Every community has untapped talents that librarians can use if only we make our needs known.

Librarians in large cities or university towns should also consider recruiting people to produce shows in languages other than English. The performance can be recorded on tape or a cassette, so we need have only one performance by the original actors. Since the action in a puppet show tells the story, children can be exposed to the text in another language and still enjoy the show. Such performances can be used to celebrate United Nations Day or holidays of other countries. No one who has watched children enjoying a puppet show in a language they do not understand can doubt the importance of this multicultural approach to library programming.

FILM PROGRAMS

When films were first introduced into libraries, they were seen as promotional gimmicks to bring new patrons into the library and to lure the people attending the programs into borrowing books. It has taken time for librarians to recognize that the film is a bonafide medium of communication.

A film program has many advantages. It can accommodate a large audience and appeal to a wide age range. Many films are available free or at very low cost, and most cooperative library systems have an extensive film library from which to select.

Most librarians have overcome their awe of film projectors as more and more library schools require knowledge of audiovisual equipment use before graduation. In addition there are self-threading projectors that remove the need for any skill.

Films serve as many purposes as books do. Some are aesthetic experiences that move the viewers to laughter or tears; some are good at provoking later discussion; and some simply convey information. Most films for children fall into the first and third categories, although some, like The Fable of He and She[3] about sex roles, can serve as the starting point for discussion.

In planning film programs the librarian must be aware of what community purpose they are to serve. If we want to entertain the children, that is fine. If we want family programming in order to attract a wide age range of people, then we need to stress that fact in our publicity. A sound knowledge of our community helps us to plan programs that meet many people's needs. For instance, in an area where many people own snowmobiles, a library film program can both entertain and inform an audience about matters of safety, courtesy, and the sport of snowmobiling. If we are located in an area where surfing is a big activity, a library program can focus on that. However, it is important to remember that people do not have to be participants in an activity to be interested in it, and showing films about snowmobiles in surfboard country may bring out a large audience. The unknown has just as strong an attraction as the familiar.

Many young people today are making their own films, and the library can sponsor programs that demonstrate different techniques of filmmaking. If there is an active young people's film club, the library can arrange to have a preview program where all the young people can show their films to the community at large.

The use of films within the library is limited only by our imagination. With so many commercial films now available, we can help children become knowledgeable critics by showing such films as *My Side of the Mountain*[4] or a Walt Disney production and having the children discuss why the film differs from the original book or story. We can help them see why some things *had* to be changed to fit the medium of film and why others were changed to alter the message.

SPECIAL PROGRAMS

All of the programs we have been talking about so far are most effective when run regularly. Regularly may mean once a week from October to May; once a month; on a six-week or eight-week cycle; every Wednesday during summer vacation—any practical arrangement, just so long as the programs have continuity.

There is, however, another type of program that is effective—the special or "one-shot" program. This may involve a local author or illustrator talking or drawing for the children; or it may involve building a program around a special interest shared by the children in the community; or it may mean a program held in cooperation with another agency in our community.

Everyone loves to meet a real live author or illustrator. The fact that those who write or illustrate books—or do both—are ordinary human beings does not matter to most people—we have an awe, all of us, whatever our ages, of the people who produce the books we cherish. Some authors write mediocre books but are compelling public speakers; some write grand books but are sleep-inducing on the rostrum. The ideal, obviously, is to find a person like Newbery Medal author Lloyd Alexander who writes well and relates well to an audience. We should attempt to find out how well an author or illustrator can speak before planning a program, but since everyone has to begin somewhere, we should not be afraid to give a new author or illustrator a first opportunity. We should be willing to share our knowledge of the most interesting speakers with other librarians in the area.

Identifying a special interest among the patrons of a library is simple: a steady run on stamp-collecting books and a continuous argument over who is next to get *Scott's Specialized Catalog of United States Stamps* informs the librarian that this may be an interest upon which to capitalize. If we are fortunate enough to have a philatelic society in our community, we can turn to it for resource people and advice on how to plan a program that includes films of foreign countries or a slide-show of rare stamps. If we do not have a philatelic society to turn to for help, we can begin simply by opening the library's meeting room on a Saturday morning for a "swap session." This will tell us how much interest there is and enable us to plan for more elaborate programs in the future.

Cooperation with other agencies can take many forms. Most police departments now run bicycle safety programs and the library can collect all its books about bicycles and invite a representative from the police department to be the speaker at a "Bike Day." Skate boarding has had a revival—if we live long enough, we encounter re-runs of most fads—and offers the possibility of a very popular program. However, librarians planning programs that involve actual bike riding or skate boarding on library property should make sure their library's insurance policy covers such activities.

One of the most elaborate and successful cooperative programs I have ever seen occurred in Halifax, Nova Scotia. It involved the staff of the Children's Hospital, the library, the school board, student nurses from three institutions, and the Women's Auxiliary of the hospital. The idea for the program began with a discussion between the hospital's Director of the Child Life Department and the children's librarian. The latter, skilled in the art of puppet shows, agreed to create a special program about what goes on at a hospital. "Dr. Goodlove," as the show was called, was performed at both the hospital (for the hospitalized children) and the library. After every show, the children were able to play with plaster casts, putting them on themselves or on dolls; they also saw a model operating table and could dress up in O.R. gowns, masks, and rubber gloves; they were able to hear a heart beat through a stethoscope, find out how the blood pressure instrument worked, and have their finger pricked for a blood sample that they were then able to see under a microscope.

Student nurses from Dalhousie University, Victoria General Hospital, and the Infirmary gave their time to help the children have these experiences. It was the first time that the three nurses' training institutions had cooperated with each other, not to mention with the library.

The Child Life Department of the hospital and the library co-sponsored a contest for children in the Halifax city schools. Children could write stories or poems, or they could draw pictures about any aspect of hospitalization. The hospital's Women's Auxiliary provided the money for prizes, which consisted of books about hospitals or some aspect of health.

Except for the specially created puppet show, none of the activities took a great deal of anyone's time. The long-term effects of the program may never be measurable, but one hopes that at least some of the children who participated will have fewer fears and be less apprehensive about any future experience with hospitalization. This was an excellent example of programming that was both fun and informative.

Many organizations in our communities have messages they wish to deliver to children. An alert children's librarian can canvass these organizations to ascertain which would be participants in cooperative programs. If it is the outside organization that makes the initial contact, librarians must, of course, be receptive to the offers.

Whether special programs originate inside or outside the library, all librarians should be aware of their value. They are the programs most likely to reach library non-users, and any time we have the opportunity to tell a new group of children that the library has an interest in them, we must take advantage of the situation.

PUBLICITY

In letting the public know what the library was up to, librarians have always been good about advertising programs within the library itself, putting posters in stores and schools, and using the local newspaper. However, when it comes to using the electronic media, our profession has been reluctant, perhaps doubting that what we were doing was important enough to be announced on radio and television. On the other hand, when the New York Public Library launched a television campaign to recruit library patrons, the public response was overwhelming. Libraries that have tried "Dial-a-Story" on the telephone have been forced to discontinue the service because they could not cope with the demand.

Such examples suggest that there are many children out there who, like adults, do not know about the library but, when exposed to its possibilities, are eager for what it has to offer.

We must learn to use public service television as well as the commercial stations. In Canada, the Canadian Broadcasting Company has abolished advertising on radio and opened up the airwaves to prime time "public service" announcements for any group willing to take advantage of its services. Access to television is not impossible to achieve, as the New York Public Library experience proved, but it is harder than obtaining radio time. Most public service announcements on television do not exceed ten seconds; it requires skill to convey a concise message in that time.

Where there is a community television station—usually referred to as a cable station—we can ask to have a story hour or preschool program taped and have the closing message tell viewers, "It's lots more fun to be there in person. Why don't you come see for yourself." This should be followed by the date and time of *one* program. A big mistake is to try and tell viewers or listeners too much. One item at a time is more productive than six, when none of the six are remembered.

Besides using the public media, librarians whose circulation systems allow them to know who borrows which books can send individual invitations to children who have borrowed books on the topic of the special program. If a program is planned far enough in advance, the staff can insert a notice of an upcoming program into books that deal with the same topic.

If the library has one person responsible for public relations, the children's librarian should make a special effort to communicate with that person and see to it that the public relations office gives good service to children's programming. If children's librarians may be said to have one overriding defect, it is our tendency to isolate ourselves from the rest of the library staff. However, if we educate other members of the staff to understand the crucial importance to the community of children's services, we will find ourselves operating in a much more productive atmosphere. Certainly, we should manage to convey what children's services are all about to the person whose job it is to reach the media.

DO-IT-THEMSELVES PROGRAMMING

While it is a responsibility for librarians to plan programs that meet the needs of children, we also have the responsibility to encourage them to plan their own programs. If the library's auditorium or meeting room is available to groups within the community, we should let children know that they can make use of the facilities on equal terms with other people.

Earlier we talked about having a film program that let young filmmakers display their creations to the community at large. But we should also let these young people know that the physical facilities are available to them if they want to have their film club meet in the library.

109

If a group of children want to put on a play, they should know that the library's facilities are open to them. They do not have to look for a family garage or attic. The children, like adult groups, should have the option of using the facilities for their own group or for having a public program.

I am talking here about children's groups that have no adult leader. An adult should not be necessary for children to have access to the library's facilities—at least not in those libraries that subscribe to the Library Bill of Rights. And just as we publicize our own programs, so should we be sure to let the children in our community know about our policy of free access to facilities for all members of the community. It is not enough to say, "Nobody ever asked." Nobody ever will unless we tell them it is possible.

NOTES FOR CHAPTER 7

1. *The Pleasure Is Mutual.* (Film) Connecticut Films Production. Children's Book Council, Inc., 1966, 25 mins.
2. *There's Something About a Story.* (Film) Connecticut Films Production. 1969, 27 mins.
3. *Fable of He and She.* (Film) Made by Eliot Noyes, Jr. Learning Corporation of America, 1974, 11 mins.
4. *My Side of the Mountain.* (Film) A Robert B. Radnitz Production. Distributed by Paramount.

CHAPTER
EIGHT

The Library and the Community

IN THE preceding chapter we were concerned with cooperation between the library and outside organizations as they affected programming. Now we turn our attention to our relationship with institutions and agencies serving children, and with adult leaders of child-centered groups. The discussion is from the viewpoint of the public library, but cooperation between school librarians and community agencies and groups can be achieved by minor adaptations in the approach.

THE SCHOOLS

Sometimes it seems as if there have been hundreds of words, thousands of words, millions and billions and trillions of words written about the relationship of the school and the public library in America. It also seems that most of the words were designed to further misunderstanding and create confusion in the mind of the reader. [1]

I wrote those words for the 1965 edition of *An Introduction to Children's Work in Public Libraries* and it is one of the few paragraphs in that book that remains as true today as when written over a decade ago. In 1970, the American Library Association issued *Bibliography of Related Books and Articles on School and Public Library Relations* [2]; in *Children's Library Service* [3] (1974)

Burke and Shields updated the ALA bibliography. The tidal wave of words goes on and nothing in practice changes.

In times of affluence, the two agencies do not feel any need to cooperate; in financial hard times, they view each other as competitors for the few tax dollars available. The conflict between school and public librarians was exacerbated when ALA changed its dues structure and required divisions to be self-supporting. This change meant that school librarians had to pay an extra fifteen dollars to belong to CSD (now ALSC) or YASD in addition to AASL (American Association of School Librarians). While the same was true for children's or young adult librarians who wanted to belong to the Public Library Association, there has never been the strong loyalty toward PLA among public library children's specialists that exists among school librarians toward AASL. Now, besides competing for local tax dollars, we are in competition within our national organization for membership dues.

It is almost impossible for state library associations to have a section or division that combines school and public librarians in any equal numbers. Some children's librarians do join a state school library association; a small percentage of school librarians join the state library association. If we cannot bring ourselves to cooperate at the professional level, is there any possibility that we can cooperate at the practical level?

As long as we do not dream about a nationwide cooperation, the answer can be yes. In individual communities on the North American continent, school and public librarians do have good relationships, but even in those communities, cooperation falls short of the dream. Ideally, there should be centralized ordering and processing for all libraries within the same governmental entity, with a union catalog for all holdings so that easy interloan procedures exist.

While awaiting utopia, there are ways in which public library children's specialists can work with the schools, whether they have a school librarian or not. The first act of a children's librarian should be to survey the number of schools served by the public library and obtain an accurate count of how many classes are in each school. One branch library in a large urban system may

113

have as many as thirty schools within its boundaries; in small towns the public library may be a single central unit without branches, while the school system has eight or ten elementary schools, with twenty or more classes in each school. Whatever the actual numbers, the public library is far outnumbered by schools.

Once the children's librarian knows how many classes there are in the public, private, and parochial schools in the area served by the public library, the next step is to divide the number of weeks in the school year (minus those weeks taken up with testing, examinations, and other set school functions) into the number of classes. This tells us how many classes would be coming to the library each week if the demand were evenly spread. But we know that there is a unit "Community Helpers" in the primary grades (generally the third grade, but can vary from school system to school system), and when that unit is being taught, all the third grade teachers will want to bring a class to the library. This means that there will be no even demand for visits to the library, so we will have to adjust our schedules accordingly.

Each class visit requires one professional librarian and one supporting staff member, over and above whatever staff is necessary for serving the general public. Thus, the number of staff a children's room has determines how many class visits may be scheduled without exhausting the staff and trying the public's patience.

All but the rarest of libraries will be short on staff, requiring the librarian to make choices among the many potential classes. The temptation, when faced with such decisions, is for the librarian to prefer to take the "A" classes over the "B" or "C" classes. A second temptation is to take those that ask to come and to ignore those whose teachers ignore us. Both temptations should be resisted. If we select the top classes within each grade level for visits to the library we are not only open to the charge of elitism but also to a charge of redundancy. The chances are a higher percentage of students in the "A" classes have library cards and use them than in the "C" classes. (It might, in fact, be worth the time to do a very simple survey of the schools to de-

114

termine what percentage of students have library cards and use the library at least once each month. Too many of our decisions are based on assumptions for which no factual verification exists.)

If we make up the schedule well in advance, we can send application forms to either the classroom teacher or the school librarian with the request they be returned a week or two before the visit. By doing this, we can have the library cards ready when the class visits and children who want to borrow materials may do so without delay. We should keep in mind that using a library is a habit and like other habits becomes stronger with each experience.

The structure of a class visit depends on the reason the class is coming. If it is coming to be introduced to the public library our approach differs from that used when the class is coming to be introduced to specific materials for a school assignment. In the former case, we should take the class to the auditorium or meeting room, get the children settled, and explain the general rules and regulations governing library behavior. It is helpful to have a slide presentation of the library, with scripts prepared with different age groups in mind since we do not want to bore sixth graders with information designed for first graders, or vice versa. A written script is a good precaution. The best of us can be ill, but with a script, anyone in the building can stand in for us. The slides help the children visualize the library and will produce a degree of recognition on the actual tour.

Depending on the time the class is scheduled to be in the library, we can have the tour, return to the auditorium, tell the children a story, and then let them browse. If time is short, we can tell an under-five-minute story and let them know when the library's regularly scheduled programs are held, take the tour, and let them browse. However we handle the visits, it is well to remember that they should not be exactly the same, but designed for the particular class coming. Just as all children differ from each other, so do all classes.

One important point of courtesy is to inform the school librarian about the titles of books we will be talking about, the story or stories we select to tell, and any other information that may

115

create a demand on the school library collection. Children will ask for the materials whenever they think of them and not distinguish between school and public library.

If the class is visiting the library because it is about to embark on a new unit of study and the teacher wants the children to have an introduction to materials the library owns on a topic, our routine will differ from the introductory visit. We will have gathered together representative items on the subject from all parts of the library. For example, if the unit is on a particular foreign country or region of the world, we will have on display in the auditorium materials from the fiction and nonfiction collections, phonodiscs of folk tales from the country or region, filmstrips, vertical file material, and periodicals. If time allows, we can end with a carefully selected film. Additional materials can be placed on one or more book trucks in the children's room, and students allowed to borrow the items, keeping in mind, however, that other classes will be studying the same unit and it is not unreasonable to limit the materials on loan to the class. We can also stress the need for sharing materials with other students and returning them as soon as possible.

Teachers who are not interested in visiting the library may be receptive to a visit by us to the classroom. This option is often considered second-best by public librarians, but I would prefer to think of it as simply an alternative, without placing it in a hierarchy. Even if the classroom teacher is aware of the need to obtain the principal's permission to have an outsider in the school, we should always take the time to write a letter saying how much we are looking forward to our visit on such and such a date to so-and-so's class. A similar letter, which includes a list of the materials we plan to discuss, should be sent to the school librarian.

When we first begin making school visits, many of us are fearful. We are moving into strange territory, and we cannot control the situation. The first time we are in the middle of a story or booktalk and the loudspeaker interrupts with a message, we are likely to be paralyzed. If we do not keep our eyes on the time, we may be startled by the bell or buzzer sounding the end of the class period and find we have all kinds of items left over. On the other hand, if we are not trained in public speaking, we may find

116

that information we thought would take a half-hour to share has been covered in ten minutes. None of these disasters brings with it the end of the world and none should deter us from trying again.

Another reason even the most experienced librarians are vaguely unhappy about making classroom visits is the lack of adequate display materials. If we have established a good relationship with the school librarian, we can ask her or him to provide the books we want to talk about and save ourselves the trouble of carrying large numbers of books—or settling for talking about too few. Paperbacks can be used in place of hardcover books: they are lighter in weight, tend to have more attractive covers, and can be supplied in multiple copies so we can satisfy the demand we are creating.

The problem of attractively displaying the public library materials we bring with us has an easy solution, taught to me by a former student. From a building supply outlet buy one four-by eight-foot sheet of half-inch Styrofoam and have it cut into two two- by four-foot pieces. Tape the edges of the pieces with colored masking tape and, using regular notebook binder rings, connect the two pieces together so they open like a book. Any lightweight library materials, such as book jackets, promotional materials, bookmarks, etc., can be attached to the Styrofoam by straight pins and the whole thing can be carried by two fingers—literally. (Joined Styrofoam boards are very inexpensive and can be used in a library setting with limited display space because they stand on their own and can be moved about. The boards can also be cut in smaller pieces and used as a backdrop for signs or for public announcements, or in the staff lounge. Get some and you'll find another hundred uses I haven't thought of yet.)

One of the reasons school and public librarians have so much trouble cooperating is that many school systems impose stringent restrictions upon their librarians. Many school librarians would love to attend the monthly meetings of public librarians in their area, but regulations force them to be in the school at all times school is in session, except for meetings called by the school library supervisor. One possible solution to this problem is for the public library children's coordinator and the school library supervisor to call joint meetings, some of which will be

117

held in the schools and some in the public libraries. Besides cementing good relations between the two groups, this technique allows both sets of librarians to see many different libraries in the area, since monthly meetings should not always be held in the same location unless absolutely necessary.

If the public librarian and the school librarian can become professional colleagues, and perhaps even friends, it will save both of them a great deal of trouble. When the public librarian has a new-books list that would interest teachers of a particular subject, the school librarian is an ideal person to see that the list reaches the right people. On the other hand, when the school librarian needs either materials or information from the public library, it is nice to have a personal contact through which to make the request.

Even if we are not able to achieve centralized purchasing and processing procedures, we can at least share our expert reviewers with each other. If the school librarian has discovered some teachers who are enthusiastic about reviewing new books, copies of the reviews could be shared with the public librarian. Similarly, the public librarian, or the library system children's consultant, should be sharing reviews with the school librarians. The development of public library cooperative systems over the past fifteen years ought to have helped improve cooperative efforts between school and public libraries, but it is still rare to find system consultants meeting regularly with the school library coordinators within their service area. While no consultant or coordinator can guarantee the cooperation of individual libraries within their respective systems, it is fair to say that the higher the level at which cooperation is initiated, the better the chance it has of being successful.

COMMUNITY GROUPS

There are two basic types of community groups or agencies that should interest the children's librarian. The first group consists of those organizations that work directly *with* children; the second group consists of organizations that work *for* children.

Most children's librarians have worked well with the groups

118

that work with children. We have established good relationships with Scouting groups, at both the local and national levels. We keep abreast of what requirements are necessary to obtain a particular badge and stand ready to assist Scout leaders with materials that will help their youthful charges qualify for those badges. Similar statements can be made about 4-H clubs, the Little League, and whatever other groups exist within our communities.

Unfortunately, our focus has been entirely on meeting the needs of the children in the particular groups and we have ignored the needs of the adult leaders. This situation exists because the materials that would help an adult become a better leader and add to the leader's understanding of children and their developmental patterns are in the adult section of the library's collection. It is absolutely essential that the children's librarian and the adult services librarian sit down together and come to an agreement about how they can coordinate their services to adults working with children. Many of our failures to give good service to community groups is based on the fact that we do not have adequate communication within the library. When our own house is in order, we stand a better chance of giving good service to adults working with young people.

Service to groups working with children should begin with top-level cooperation. The tendency to work with the individual leader is strong, but for every leader who thinks of the public library as a resource there may be six who do not. If we sit down with the district executive officer and analyze the types of services we can offer, they can be packaged once by us and the district executive can then assume responsibility for having the package reach all leaders.

We should keep in mind that there are two types of groups working with children in our communities: (1) volunteer agencies, and (2) public agencies. We do better with the former than the latter. One of the most important public agencies is the recreation department. In some towns, the recreation department has a "Fun Mobile," which travels a circuit the same way library bookmobiles do, bringing all types of recreational activities to widely dispersed sections of the community.

The Fun Mobile may stop at playgrounds, church halls, or housing projects, depending on the facilities available in the different sections of town. For indoor stops, the library can provide films; the librarian can put on a puppet show; or, if the rec department is sponsoring a demonstration by a craft artist, the librarian can provide a booklist and a display of books about the craft.

For decades, children's librarians have been visiting playgrounds during the summer and telling stories, but there are so many other ways in which we can cooperate with the recreation department that we should not stop there, and perhaps we should not even give storytelling top priority. For example, if the library sponsors a video club, the members might tape events such as local ball games or track and field competitions. Showing the tapes in the library ought to attract a fair sized audience.

One of the major complaints social critics have of our society is that children are overprogrammed. If the library and the recreation department work together, we can cut down on duplication of services and not place ourselves in the position of competing for the attention of the children. On the contrary, both agencies will be in a better position to demonstrate to the budget committee that each is doing what it does best and that in cooperating the two together are accomplishing more than either could separately.

AGENCIES WORKING FOR CHILDREN

Agencies working for children also work with some children, but the distinction between these agencies and the groups discussed above is that the children they see directly are not there voluntarily. Social workers, for example, may deal with children whose families are on welfare; public health nurses may be working with children who have been physically abused; people in the juvenile justice system see children assigned to them by the courts.

Libraries have much to offer these and other agencies in the community. Child abuse, for example, is finally being discussed openly in society. Both the social work and public health departments are concerned with the problem and should welcome an opportunity to cosponsor a series of programs on the subject. An advantage to this approach to a very difficult social problem is that the library can offer it as a general information program without labeling the people who attend it as having the problem. The entire community has a vested interest in the subject, and the program should be advertised on those terms.

The children's librarian can put together the books in the children's collection that have child abuse as their subject, the adult services librarian can gather the books for adults, and the agencies can select the speakers and determine the format of the program (whether one night is enough or whether a series is necessary). Here again, we should use our competencies to complement the competencies of other agencies.

Involvement with the people in the juvenile justice system requires an across-the-board approach, and libraries fortunate enough to have a young adult services librarian will certainly want to include her or him. There is a movement toward removing young people from the large, impersonal institutional settings and establishing them in houses with a couple serving as surrogate parents. More than any other youth in our society, these children and teenagers need help in learning to operate successfully in the outside world. If such houses are being established in our communities, our first step might be to offer each home a collection of paperback books. While not engaging in actual bibliotherapy (an action I disapprove of by untrained therapists), we can offer to hold discussion groups in the home. As the young people acquire self-confidence, we can ask if they would not like to participate in the discussions held in the library.

Anything we can do to help these young people caught in the juvenile justice system to become part of the activities of the library is worth doing. They need to meet and interact with other children or teenagers who are not in legal trouble so they can see that there are other ways of coping with problems. We should also remember that many of these young people are not trapped in the legal system for having committed crimes.

We should let the surrogate parents of these young people

121

know that we stand ready to help them. They may want books about youth living in institutional settings; they may want to be kept abreast of new adult books on the subject of handling difficult children. Whatever the particular needs of the surrogate parents, they should learn to look to the library for help—if only for the opportunity to borrow 8- or 16-millimeter films for showing at home.

If our community is still locking youth up in a large institution we should make it our business to discover what library facilities the institution offers. Except for the rare institution, the chances are that library facilities are nonexistent or of very poor quality. It may be that we can put a collection of paperbacks in the day room or social room (whatever it is called), so the children have free access to books during their free periods. If our puppet theater stage is portable, we might be able to put on a monthly program for the children, and perhaps even encourage them to write a script and make the puppets for their own show. The opportunities are unlimited and only time and money impose restrictions upon them.

The same may be said for working with groups within the community. No library has the staff or resources to work at the same high level of cooperation with all groups. Which ones we select to work with and which we ignore will be based on our value system and our personal characteristics. Some very good librarians are uncomfortable working with people in trouble; others are unhappy working with white, middle-class youngsters. Since none of us can do everything, we must make choices. We need not feel guilty about the choices as long as we are aware that there are unmet needs in the community and seek to hire personnel who can work with the groups that make us uncomfortable.

NOTES FOR CHAPTER 8

1. Dorothy M. Broderick, *An Introduction to Children's Work in Public Libraries*, New York: H. W. Wilson, 1965, p. 84.
2. *Bibliography of Related Books and Articles on School and Public Library Relations*, Chicago: American Library Association, 1970.
3. J. Gordon Burke, and Gerald R. Shields, *Children's Library Service*, Metuchen, NJ: Scarecrow Press, 1974.

CHAPTER
NINE

Areas Related to Work With Children

To BE a good librarian, it is not enough to have a command of library literature and materials for children; we must also be aware of and become knowledgeable in areas of such diverse fields as psychology, ethics, and television. In this chapter, I want to identify some of the most important of these areas. These overviews will not make anyone an expert but are designed to alert librarians to related disciplines that should be part of our general background knowledge.

JEAN PIAGET

It is impossible to overstate the importance of Jean Piaget's work in the field of child development. After decades of being ignored by psychologists and educators in North America, Piaget's work now provides the underpinning for almost all research being done into the cognitive and moral development of children.

For a librarian a grasp of Piaget is essential for understanding Lawrence Kohlberg's theory of moral development and the entire approach to moral education currently being developed (discussed in the following section). The research by Bever *et al.* on children's reactions to tv commercials (discussed later in the chapter) also has as its basis of analysis Piaget's theory of cognitive development. The establishment of a library program for teaching children about death (also discussed in this chapter) re-

124

quires a good understanding of Piaget. In short, while we can grasp much of what researchers of children's development are telling us without knowing Piaget, our appreciation will be enhanced, and our library programs will benefit, if we have a general knowledge of his theories.

Piaget began his career by studying psychology, with its emphasis on the pathological and its related concern for psychoanalysis. Those approaches did not interest him, however. He preferred normality over pathology, and "the workings of the intellect to . . . the tricks of the unconscious."[1] So he set out simply to observe children and record their actions, their patterns of reasoning, and their use of language.

While Piaget's works were available in English before 1930, they found little acceptance in North America because, as David Elkin explains in his introduction to *Jean Piaget: The Man and His Ideas:*

> . . . traditional psychology had always defined learning as "the modification of behavior as the result of experience."
>
> Such a definition makes the learner a more or less passive recipient of environmental happenings. While this may be true of rats, it is certainly not true of children. Piaget turned the definition around and spoke of learning as, in part, "the modification of experience as the result of behavior." He argued that the child's actions upon the world changed the nature of his experience. . . . Human experience, then, must be relative to human action.
>
> This theory has been one of the most difficult for American educators and psychologists to accept, even those who are sympathetic to Piaget's views. It has been difficult to accept because of a lack of familiarity with Piaget's third principle of mental growth. *Our tradition has been one of empiricism, which assumes a complete separation of mind and reality. Implicit in empiricism is a kind of "copy" theory of learning that says that our minds simply copy what exists in the outside world, much as a photograph copies the light patterns conveyed to the exposed film. Piaget argues that the mind never copies reality but instead organizes it and transforms it, reality, in and of itself, being—as Kant made clear —unknowable.*[2] (emphasis added)

125

Another confusion many of us suffer from is equating thought with language:

> Piaget's general position seems to be that thought can neither be reduced to language nor explained by it. Thought cannot be reduced to language, since, when language is absent, as in the case of the deaf, thought can still be shown to exist. Likewise thought cannot be explained by language because the linguistic conquest of rational tasks follows, rather than proceeds, their resolution on the plane of action. More particularly, thought and language seem to have different origins. Thought derives from the abstraction of one's own actions upon things. Ordering objects, putting them into groups, transforming them in multiple ways by motor manipulations provide the basis for those abstractions which become mental operations. Language, on the other hand, is derived from experiences which are not a product of the child's own activity but are rather imitations of patterns provided by adults. It is this difference in origin which accounts for the fundamental duality between thought and language.[3]

Piaget offers so many practical situations which lend themselves to replication that any of us with access to children can verify his findings. It is important to remember that although individual children may advance through the stages of cognitive development at varying rates—some slower, some faster—all children will pass through all the stages, *if they are provided with appropriate learning situations.* In Piaget's terms, an appropriate learning situation is "a mixture of direction and freedom."[4] It is a situation in which the adult may pose the problem but the child provides the answer—and provides it without correction by an adult who wishes the child to see "the answer" in the same light the adult does.

At the most practical level, Piaget offers insights that can be useful to librarians in evaluating the "appropriateness" of materials for children. For example, a reading of Piaget's *The Child's Conception of Physical Causality*[5] might lead us to conclude that while we may enjoy the easy-to-read science books for the under-eight-year-olds, these books simply impose an adult understanding of the world upon children. In this connection, it is instructive to see the results of Piaget's experiments with children in relation to such topics as *What is wind?* and *Where does it come from?*

It would be most useful in a library to have available those books that contain Piaget-type experiments, so that teachers, parents, and librarians could pose the problems to children and see how far they had progressed in their understanding of the physical world. We would then be in a position to choose materials that take the children one small step ahead, since the process of giving up erroneous views of the world is dependent upon the child having enough experiences (and reading is one of them) to come to recognize that a currently-held view is wrong.

We might also see how inappropriate are those beautifully illustrated picture books of Aesop's fables and other stories that rely on an appreciation of metaphor for full understanding. Piaget maintains that it is not until adolescence that appreciation of books like *Gulliver's Travels* and *Alice's Adventures in Wonderland* can occur, because only then do young people acquire the ability to deal with symbolic rather than concrete knowledge.[6]

In the traditional views expressed in library literature (represented by such works on books for young people as *An Ample Field*[7] and *Longer Flight*[8]), the fact that adolescents may borrow *Wind in the Willows* and *Crime and Punishment* simultaneously is seen simply as an indication that the children are torn between their desire to move into adulthood and their need to retain the dependence of childhood. Piaget's theory offers a deeper, more complex, and psychologically more realistic explanation: the "juvenile" books—in this case *The Wind in the Willows*—that adolescents return to are those that can be read at *several* levels. The young people have reached a stage of development where they are now ready to enjoy nuances of character motivation as well as plots, having acquired the appreciation of metaphor, allusion, and *double entendre* that will enrich another reading of Grahame as well as illuminate the complexities of Dostoevsky.

Reading Piaget provides many other insights into the developmental process and can make us better at our jobs.

KOHLBERG AND MORAL EDUCATION

The idea of what constitutes morality has intrigued philosophers and theologians as long as the human race has had the time to contemplate. In recent years, it has become a major concern of developmental psychologists and educational psychologists.

For many people, morality is directly connected with religion. And when a discussion of "moral education" is introduced, they see it as a threat to religious beliefs. Alternatively, those who oppose any religious education may see moral education as a backdoor attempt to slide religion into school curricula. Both groups have in common the mistaken notion that religion provides the basis for morality.

Early researchers into notions of morality shared a similar view—they operated on the assumption that there are "rights" and "wrongs" in personal behavior that are not only universal but totally consistent. For example, in theory it ought to follow that "having respect for the law" means that someone would: (1) never rob a bank, (2) always be truthful in filling out the income tax form, (3) obey all traffic regulations, and (4) come to the aid of the police in time of trouble. Also in theory, it ought to follow that if children do not cheat on a test, despite being given the opportunity, they will also tell the truth and play according to the rules of the game.

The theory of consistency in personal behavior sounded logical, but it could not be verified by researchers. As Lawrence Kohlberg observed:

> The earliest major psychological study of moral character, that of Hugh Hartshorne and Mark May in 1928–1930, focused on a bag of virtues including honesty, service (altruism or generosity), and self-control. To their dismay, they found that there were *no* character traits, psychological dispositions, or entities which corresponded to words like honesty, service, or self-control.[9]

The early research focused on what people ought to do rather than their *reasons* for behaving as they actually do. For example, while cheating is frowned upon by most people, if children have absorbed the idea that receiving good grades is more important than failing honestly, then they may cheat. The goal of good grades takes priority over the way in which the grades are achieved. Once we understand this, we can see that for the child, the moral question here involves the traditional dilemma of whether worthy goals justify unworthy means.

In *The Moral Judgment of the Child*[10], Jean Piaget laid the foundation for present-day research by pointing out that for children under eight years, all rules are heteronomous—that is, they are imposed by adult authority. Older children, on the other hand, begin to internalize a respect for rules, and, most important, operate as though the rules of a game represented a contract among the players. Because young children have no internalized concept of the "rules of the game," they can happily vary the rules as the urge strikes them. As anyone is aware who has watched a five-year-old and a nine-year-old play a game together, it is quite likely that the nine-year-old will become angry about what he or she views as outrageous cheating by the younger child. Piaget would say that cheating is an inappropriate word, since it presumes the deliberate breaking of an unspoken contract, which is a concept the five-year-old cannot know.

Taking Piaget's work as a starting point, Lawrence Kohlberg began a longitudinal study of the moral values of children and young people. (See bibliography for a selection of Kohlberg's writings.) Instead of asking children questions for which our society ordains a "right" or a "wrong" answer, Kohlberg presented the children with moral dilemmas for which there are no preordained correct answers.

Kohlberg's research has resulted in a theory of moral development that identifies three levels, each of which has two stages and more than thirty "aspects" as last count. Level one is termed "preconventional morality," and at the first stage, the child's morality is based on fear of punishment; at the second stage, it is based on the promise of rewards, and Kohlberg calls the resulting behavior "naive instrumental hedonism."

Level two is "conventional morality," and its first stage is "good boys do this, good girls do that"; the second-stage morality is based on a respect for authority, whether secular or religious.

Before moving onto a description of level three, let me make clear Kohlberg's distinction between fear of punishment and respect for authority. Faced with a dilemma that has as one solution the breaking of a law, a child at the first stage of level one will argue that breaking the law is wrong because if you get caught you will be put in jail. A child at the second stage of level two will reason that you do not break the law because laws are necessary for the smooth running of society.

In one way or another all stages in the first two levels represent the acceptance of externally imposed values, with the stages in level two being prime examples of social conditioning that leads to conformity. At level three, termed "postconventional morality," the moral arguments are based on self-accepted principles. The first stage of level three represents the "social contract" idea that if everyone broke the laws he or she did not like, society would be in a mess. The second stage is based on the person's conscience.

One of the important conclusions Kohlberg reached is that six people, each at a different stage, can decide to take the same action, and that it is only their reasons for doing so that distinguish their moral stages.

Like other stage-sequence theories, Kohlberg maintains that we must proceed through them in order. One may not skip a stage. Nor is it possible for us to understand the reasoning of a stage more than one level above the stage we are at, but we *can* understand the reasoning (although rejecting it) for all stages we have passed through. Finally, because Kohlberg worked with youth in Taiwan, Mexico, Turkey, and Great Britain, he has stated that his theory is not culturally limited.

There are flaws in Kohlberg's theory, just as there are flaws in all theories dealing with human behavior since people are so complex it is probably impossible to construct any system that accounts for all human variability. However, the flaws do not mean that we have to toss the entire theory out; on the contrary, the flaws have stimulated so much additional research that they have a definite catalytic value. To keep on top of the research being done in moral development theories, all librarians should read regularly the *Journal of Moral Education*[11].

There are many practical applications of Kohlberg's theory for librarians. For example, it is helpful for a librarian who is explaining to children why they should conform to the library's rules to know that younger children are more likely to accept the punishment–reward reasoning, while older children can be reasoned with in terms of "the right thing to do," or general respect for authority.

In areas where courses in moral education have been introduced into the school system, both school and public librarians may be called upon to recommend books that will lend themselves to discussion in class. To do that job well we have to have a basic knowledge of the levels of moral development. Then we must begin to categorize books in a new way, according to the *reasons* characters behave as they do.

Knowledge of moral stages also can help us defend the newer sex education materials. The older titles were firmly rooted in level two, stage one: "good boys do this, good girls do that." Newer materials are based on level-three reasoning, with mutuality and conscience as guides to behavior. If we keep in mind what Kohlberg tells us—that people cannot grasp the reasoning of a stage more than one step above their own—we can see why people whose moral development stopped at the "good boys . . . good girls" stage are angered and confused by level-three reasoning.

We cannot assume that librarians are a special breed of human being who can achieve (collectively) stage-six reasoning. Through a reading of Kohlberg's theory, we should each be able to determine our own level simply by giving our own answers to the moral dilemmas presented by Kohlberg before reading his analysis of the children's answers. If we find that we *consistently* fall below stage-five reasoning—it is important to realize that we may operate at different stages for different dilemmas—then we should recognize that we are not the best people to defend such books as Pomeroy's *Boys and Sex* and *Girls and Sex*. Moreover, it is also vital to understand that children using the public library's children's room and those in elementary schools are far too young to grasp stage-five reasoning and that the presence of books that deal with mutuality and individual conscience as the appropriate basis for sexual behavior may be another example of imposing adult values on children.

Kohlberg's theory is fascinating, but in its complexity it tends to raise more questions than it provides answers for. People who want rigid rules that can be applied in all situations will find themselves very uncomfortable with Kohlberg.

DEATH AND MORAL EDUCATION

One of Kohlberg's major "aspects" concerns the value people put on human life, and by implication their views of death. No area in moral education is more closely connected with religion in children's books than death.

Death in children's books has an interesting history. In the earliest days, it was the most important subject. One of the earliest books for children was entitled:

> A Token for Children: being an Exact Account of the Conversion, Holy and Exemplary Lives, and Joyful Deaths of several young children. To which is now added, Prayers and Graces, fitted for the use of little Children.[12]

In commenting on this book, Zena Sutherland wrote: "To be happy meant to be secure in the avoidance of Hell and in the assurance of Heaven. Unfortunately their method of instilling religious ideas was chiefly through the use of fear—the fear of Hell."[13]

This pattern continued until the last third of the nineteenth century. As Anne Scott MacLeod observed:

> Like poverty, death was a common feature in the children's fiction before 1860; children were schooled to consider life itself as the least certain of blessings. The literature was studded with reflections upon the brevity of human life, and the consequent wisdom of making the spiritual most of the time available. . . .

132

The death of a parent, sometimes of both parents, formed the dramatic base of many tales, which then went on to relate how the children coped with their situation, bereft of the guidance and protection of a parent's care. The frequency with which this one simple plot was used suggests how convenient it was for displaying the moral lessons the authors wanted to convey. The importance of parental love and protection was dramatized by its loss; the importance of parental teaching was demonstrated by how well the orphaned child was able to manage on his own.[14]

It is not accidental that MacLeod's study ends with 1860. After that date, there were, of course, *some* examples of death in children's books, but the emphasis shifted to the Horatio Alger materialism, where success was no longer judged by the chances the character had of attaining Heaven but by the financial success obtained on earth. So much emphasis was placed on earthly success that to write of death was deemed morbid.

However prevalent death was in the early books, it must be pointed out that it was always used to preach a message and never as a topic for engaging the reader's emotional commitment to life. In recent years, thanks in part to the influence of Elisabeth Kubler-Ross, death has become a topic to be treated in children's literature without euphemisms or as an excuse for religious sermons. Death is treated with sensitivity and dignity, as the natural end to life, in such books as Paige Dixon's *May I Cross Your Golden River?* for teenagers and for very young children in Richard Kennedy's picture book, *Come Again in the Spring.*

Children's librarians should read Kubler-Ross's *On Death and Dying*[15] as a part of their professional education, if for no other reason than to recognize how unacceptable such books as Ben Shecter's *Across the Meadow* are, in comparison to the Kennedy book. Similarly, contrasting John Gunther's *Death Be Not Proud* (1949) with Dixon's *May I Cross Your Golden River?* (1975) and Doris Lund's *Eric* (1974) can show us the truth of Kubler-Ross's theory of the stages which dying patients must go through to achieve acceptance of death. In the Gunther book, young Johnny is forced to face dying on his own; his parents, doctors, and the hospital personnel spend all their time pretending he is not dying. In contrast, Jordan's death in *May I Cross Your Golden River?* and Eric's death in *Eric* are perfect examples of the peace acceptance of death brings both to the person dying and the people who must go on living.

A history of the treatment of death in children's literature would require an entire book, but it is interesting to observe that literature's maturation seems to follow the individual human pattern spelled out by Kohlberg. The literature began with books that present death in terms of fear of hell—Kohlberg's stage one—and progressed through stage two—reward of life in heaven—and in recent books is now presented in terms of stage five.

An excellent book that takes Kubler-Ross's principles and translates them to meet the needs of children is *Discussing Death: A Guide to Death Education.*[16] It is a detailed syllabus for introducing death into the curriculum, beginning with five-year-olds. It recommends both book and audiovisual materials, most of which ought to be in both public and school libraries. One of the best features of the book is that it shows how the subject of death should be integrated into the total curriculum and not developed as a separate, labeled course. This approach places a great demand on the librarian to help teachers integrate the subject, and we can fulfill that obligation only if we have sufficient understanding of the topic.

Helping children understand death seems especially important when we see how the topic is handled on television.

TELEVISION AND CHILDREN

Most of us are aware that television programming contains a large amount of violence, but that general impression becomes vividly real when we learn that by the age of fourteen the average North American child has seen about 18,000 human beings killed on television. Characters on television shows are killed to allow private detectives or police officers to find their murderers. Rarely is the death of a person made a moving, emotionally involving event. Children see performers die one week and resurface in another show the next week. Social critics who see a lessening of the value of human life in our society feel that television breeds insensitivity and encourages children to take violence as a behavior model.

While researchers struggle in vain to determine whether reading affects behavior, there is a growing body of research in television viewing that makes it increasingly difficult to ignore the idea that television viewing does influence behavior and perceptions of the world. This appears to be true of adults as well as children, Gerbner and Gross observed in "The Scary World of TV's Heavy Viewer."[17] Gerbner and Gross found that people who view television for six or more hours per day are more suspicious of other people and more afraid of encountering violence in real life than those who view less television. The findings held regardless of education, sex, and age of viewer.

As Wilbur Schramm, one of the pioneer researchers of the affects of television, stated:

> Any experience that commands so large a part of the child's time, absorbs and involves him so deeply, and leads him to identify as much as it does must play some part in shaping the kind of child who comes to school, his interests, the breadth of his world, his status figures, his vocabulary, his ability to learn from pictures and the spoken word, and his capacity for being interested or bored.[18]

Recent surveys show that as many as one-quarter of elementary school children view television for more hours of the day than they attend school. Teachers observe that many of the "spontaneous" games on the school playground are the acting out of popular television shows. And while the children today are more physically aggressive in the playground, they are more passive in learning situations, probably because they are used to having their information handed to them, rather than having to work at acquiring it.

A major study by Bever, Smith, Bengen, and Johnson, "Young Viewers' Troubling Response to TV Ads,"[19] indicates that television viewing may be interfering with the cognitive process as well as forcing children to cope with social hypocrisy in their preadolescent years. The researchers found that by exposing children to tv ads that are dishonest, we may be "permanently distorting their views of morality, society, and business." The distrust inspired by television commercials appears to carry over into a general mistrust of all authority. The implications of this study are serious. No doubt it will be the starting point for many studies in the future.

Besides the dishonesty of commercials and the large amount of violence, the sexism on television is blatant. *Channeling Children: Sex Stereotyping on Prime-Time TV* [20] is a good place to begin acquiring an understanding of the depth of sexism presented on television.

Every children's librarian should scan each issue of the *Journal of Communication*.[21] From time to time, an entire issue is devoted to studies about the effects of television on children and adolescents, and each issue contains book reviews and summaries of studies of interest to anyone concerned with the communication process.

Librarians cannot ignore television. It influences the demands made on us for materials, it influences the attitudes and behavior patterns of the children we work with, and it is a competitor for the time of the children we hope to reach.

Moreover, as society comes to accept such concepts as "the children's hour," during which adult viewing is sacrificed for the supposed welfare of the children, it just may come to assume that similar sacrifices must be required in other media, thus infringing the rights of adults as well as seriously limiting the rights of youth. For instance, at a public hearing in Timmins, Ontario, before the Ontario Royal Commission on Violence in the Communications Industry, the local branch of the Canadian Mental Health Association advocated curfews for people under sixteen, identification cards for everyone eighteen or over, and "adults only" sections in libraries as well as bookstores. Although the brief submitted did not carry the approval of the national office of the CMHA, it is nevertheless disturbing to see a branch of such a prestigious organization advocating these measures. We ignore such indicators at our own risk.

If we want to keep libraries free of such legal restrictions, we

136

have to become knowledgeable about the effects of different media on young people. We cannot lump books, magazines, comic books, radio, television, and recordings into one package and talk about them as if they were interchangeable. We have to distinguish between the media of private communication (e.g., between a book and a reader) and the mass media, and see how they differ in effect. Then we should develop library programs to explain the difference to the people in our communities.

It may be that we will have to accept more restrictive measures governing the content of television programs than are theoretically desirable in a democracy, just as we have come to accept movie code ratings. If that is the case, then it is absolutely essential that libraries remain places where patrons can encounter attitudes and ideas that are outside the mainstream represented by the mass media. Children's librarians have a responsibility to share their special knowledge of children with the entire profession—to create within their libraries that vital learning situation that Piaget called "a mixture of direction and freedom"—so that we do not develop into a society where the well-being of the average ten-year-old becomes a rationale for limiting every citizen's right to information or entertainment.

NOTES FOR CHAPTER 9

1. Richard I. Evans, *Jean Piaget; The Man and His Ideas*, translated by Eleanor Duckworth, New York: Dutton, 1973, pp. 106–7.
2. *Ibid.* p. xxxv.
3. Jean Piaget, *Six Psychological Studies*, translated by Anita Tenzer, New York: Vintage Bks, 1968, p. xvi.
4. Evans, *op. cit.*, p. 53.
5. Jean Piaget, *A Child's Conception of Physical Causality*, translated by Marjorie Gabain, Totowa, NJ: Rowman & Littlefield, 1960.
6. Evans, *op. cit.*, p. xxxiii.
7. Amelia H. Munson, *An Ample Field: Books and Young People*, Chicago: ALA, 1950.
8. Annis Duff, *Longer Flight: A Family Grows Up Through Books*, New York: Viking, 1955.
9. Lawrence Kohlberg, "The Child As Moral Philosopher," *Psychology Today*, July 1968, p. 26.
10. Jean Piaget, *The Moral Development of the Child*, translated by Marjorie Gabain, New York: Free Press, 1965.
11. *Journal of Moral Education*, NFER Publishing Company, Ltd., 2, Jennings Buildings, Thames Avenue, Windsor, Berks SL4 1QS, England.
12. Zena Sutherland, and May Hill Arbuthnot, *Children and Books*, 5th ed., Glenview, IL: Scott, 1977, p. 40.
13. *Ibid.*
14. Anne Scott MacLeod, *A Moral Tale; Children's Fiction and American Culture 1820–1860*, Hamden, CT: Archon Bks, 1975, p. 60.
15. Elisabeth Kubler-Ross, *On Death and Dying*, New York: Macmillan, 1969.
16. Gretchen C. Mills, *et al.*, *Discussing Death; A Guide to Death Education*, Homewood, IL: ETC Pubns, 1976.
17. George Gerbner, and Larry Gross, "The Scary World of TV's Heavy Viewer," *Psychology Today*, April 1976, pp. 41+.
18. Wilbur Schramm, *et al.*, *Television in the Lives of Our Children*, Stanford, CA: Stanford Univ. Press, 1961.
19. T. G. Bever, *et al.* "Young Viewers' Troubling Response to TV Ads," *"Harvard Business Review*, November/December 1975, pp.109–20.
20. *Channeling Children; Sex Stereotyping in Prime-Time TV*, Princeton, NJ: Women on Words and Images, 1975.
21. *Journal of Communication*, see particularly "TV's Effects on Children and Adolescents," Autumn, 1975.

CHAPTER
TEN

Continuing Professional Education

A MASTER'S degree from an accredited library school program is only the first step to becoming a professional librarian. No amount of schooling, however good, can prepare us for all the variables that exist in the work world. We can—and do—learn a great deal on the job, especially if we are fortunate to begin our careers in a good library system with a superior coordinator or consultant to guide us. However, most continuing education must be self-motivated to be effective.

Continuing education is not just a matter of reading new professional books and current journals. It is a matter of exploring new concepts being developed in the related areas discussed in the preceding chapter; it is reading new children's books and viewing films and listening to recordings; it is reading adult books on the topics being treated in children's materials; and it is the systematic exploration of a particular topic (or topics) so that we gradually acquire a level of expertise in subjects that directly or indirectly influence our professional performance.

Continuing education is all of the above—and something more. The development of ourselves as persons, with particular emphasis on our own code of ethics.

ETHICS IN LIBRARIANSHIP

What little discussion there is about ethics in librarianship ignores the role that ethics play in our decision-making processes.

One definition of ethics is the science of morals, the study of proper human behavior. In the context of this chapter, ethics has to do with decisions we make based on our valuing some human beings over others.

First, let me give an example from the field of health care. Suppose a government is faced with the decision of whether to spend two million dollars on a urology unit so that six patients suffering from kidney failure can have the dialysis machines they need to stay alive. The same two million dollars could be used to establish community health clinics and educate thousands of people in the prevention of illness. Whichever choice is made, the decision is an ethical one because it involves the weighing of human lives.

In librarianship, we may not face problems of life and death, but we do weigh the worth of humans and decide some are worthier than others. Traditionally, we spend more money on the business and technology section of the library than on the children's room. Frequently, we put well-built libraries in rich areas and give the ghettoes store-front branches. Too frequently, we decide that certain people—for instance, the rich, the successful, the articulate—are better to have as patrons than the poor, the struggling, and the inarticulate. These decisions are usually talked about in social and economic terms, yet they are really ethical decisions.

Not so long ago, people in social work, public health nurses, and other service professionals took the position that physical child abuse, while deplorable, was not their business. Today, the prevention of child abuse has become a major goal for these groups. At the moment, the American Library Association subscribes to the view that parents have the right to control their children's access to information. When I ask, "If it is wrong to assault a child physically, is it not equally wrong to assault that child mentally?" the answer from the profession is "Too bad, but not our business." This is an ethical attitude, which is based on the assumption that biological parents' rights are more important than children's rights.

I feel strongly that librarians should examine the recent developments in other service professions to understand how other

140

groups have moved from acceptance of what *is* to a position of advocacy of what *ought to be*. A sense of ethics is vital if such movement is to occur and such knowledge should be high on our list of priorities.

PROFESSIONAL PARTICIPATION

A large number of librarians seem to view joining library associations as an unneeded luxury. This is an unperceptive point of view.

No matter how much of a "self-starter" each of us is, the fact remains that we need stimulation. No one can be creative or knowledgeable in all areas; professional colleagues with skills that differ from ours contribute much to our continuing education.

Some librarians also feel that belonging to their local organization should have priority over membership in the American Library Association. Yet this point of view ignores vital facts in our profession: the improved status of librarianship in the last two decades is due directly to the activities of the American Library Association; the growth in the number of schools willing to hire professionally educated librarians is a direct result of ALA's American Association of School Librarians; only a strong national organization of librarians can present an effective voice to the federal government for financial support of libraries. Put in terms of self-interest, membership in ALA is an investment in our professional future that will achieve better salaries, library buildings that are a pleasure to work in, and an improved professional image in our communities.

One of the reasons so few librarians appreciate how much they can gain from membership in ALA and by attendance at the annual conference is that no one tells us how to get the most out of a conference. We tend to think that our own division's program meetings should be our first priority, but while often interesting and stimulating, such programs are only the tip of the iceberg. Now that most divisional committee meetings are open to all observers, there is a wide range of professional knowledge available to us. For instance, we can learn a great deal from watching the ALSC'S Notable Books for Children Committee discuss the books under consideration.

It may be even more useful to sit in on meetings outside our specialty. The programs and committee meetings of Library Administration Division (LAD) provide an ideal opportunity to see what issues are of concern to administrators and also to acquire the special language of librarianship that will enable us to communicate effectively with our administrators.

Some knowledge of the Young Adult Services Division (YASD) is vital to children's librarians. First, we should know as many young adult librarians as possible since they are the people who will inherit the children we have spent years with. Many, if not most, young adult librarians have very little knowledge of children's materials and while they may have a clear idea of where they want the "bridge" of YA services to mesh with the adult collection, they often have no idea of where it should connect with the children's collection. Another reason for a working knowledge of YA services is so that when a child no longer finds his or her needs met in the children's room, we have an idea of the materials in the young adult section and can provide some guidance. This is particularly important in libraries that have not yet recognized the need for a YA librarian.

Finally, when attending an ALA conference, we should sit through at least one meeting of Council to see what issues are being raised there. The debate is not always stimulating—or even to the point—but identification of the issues is.

After membership in ALA, the next level of professional involvement should be at the state or regional level. State library meetings are, of course, smaller than ALA's and thus allow us to meet more people and do more things. They offer us the opportunity to exchange experiences with people who share a similar economic, social, and cultural environment. You may even get to see how some communities within a state experience little or no trouble with would-be censors while others a few miles down the road are deep in a community-wide dispute. The librarians in these communities can shed light on ways to avoid—or ways to ask for—trouble.

Besides membership in professional associations, the good librarians must participate in workshops. These need not be primarily library-oriented workshops—in fact they probably ought not to be. Such groups as Planned Parenthood often sponsor workshops on children's sexuality that can be very useful to the librarian. Groups working with mentally retarded or handicapped children often hold meetings that can offer much to a librarian.

A JOB OR A CAREER?

It is possible to be a very competent children's librarian without becoming a specialist. The choice is ours and which we elect depends on the kind of person we are. There is a basic division between those who want a satisfying job and those who want a career. The division is a natural one and should pose no problem as long as those who want careers do not disparage the aspirations of those who want jobs and vice versa. The world needs both types of people; both should be respected.

Whatever you choose for the future, you must start by becoming a competent children's librarian, so let us look first at what is involved. Most of the periodicals discussed in Chapter 5 publish articles and library news in addition to reviews. A good librarian scans all editorial content and reads carefully major articles. Special attention should be paid to changes in editors since the tone of a periodical changes according to the personality of the editor.

In addition to the review sources already discussed, the good librarian reads *Top of the News*, [1] which comes with membership in either the Association for Library Services to Children or the Young Adult Services Division of the American Library Association. *TON*, as it is known in professional circles, is a quarterly covering both children's and young adult services. It contains a wide range of interests from creative puppetry to trends on the international scene. It also publishes selective bibliographies of films, phonodiscs, and print materials.

The most exciting periodical in the field is *Children's Literature in Education*. [2] This quarterly is international in scope, and while its main emphasis is on the literary quality of children's literature, it also deals with the social and political content of children's books.

143

There are still too many public librarians who feel that publications from the field of education are of marginal interest to them. Yet, *Language Arts*[3] and *English Journal*,[4] both published by the National Council of Teachers of English, are filled with excellent articles that analyze the content of children's and young adult books in ways that are important to all librarians. Editorially, they defend the rights of the young to read, while calling for adult leadership to provide guidance. The book reviews are of high quality.

Children's librarians not only tend to ignore materials from the field of education, but also pay scant attention to many areas of their own profession. For a children's librarian to read nothing but current literature about children's work is an act of navel gazing. It is far more important to read *Library Journal*[5] than *School Library Journal*[6]; it is more important to read the *Wilson Library Bulletin*[7] than *Horn Book.*[8] This does not mean that *SLJ* and *Horn Book* are unimportant, but rather that children's work is only a part of the profession and librarians who do not understand what is going on in the total universe of librarianship cannot operate with maximum effect.

BECOMING A CHILDREN'S SPECIALIST

When I use the word specialist, I am not talking about someone who knows *everything* about children's literature or children's services. That is an unattainable goal. A children's specialist has, however, read far more broadly in the field than most librarians, with the main purpose of selecting one or more *specific* areas in which to specialize.

The general study of children's work that must precede the more advanced investigation is most important. In our field we cannot do better than to begin our general reading with Virginia Haviland's *Children's Literature: A Guide to Reference Sources* (1966, 1972).[9] The two-volume work begins with a section called "History and Criticism," which is valuable if we want to know where we have been before deciding where to go. Simply reading the critical annotations of the works described is an education.

Where we begin in a historical investigation depends on what type of knowledge we have gained in library school. Some courses in children's literature stress the history of the subject, while others barely mention it, except as it directly relates to the discussion of current books. If one is starting from scratch, one probably should read *A Critical History of Children's Literature* by Cornelia Meigs, *et al.* [10] I say "probably," because I find it an unsatisfactory reading experience, containing numerous titles and authors but leaving me with little feel for the vitality of children's literature.

My personal bias is for a good book on a limited subject rather than for overviews. Therefore, I find Darton's *Children's Books in England: Five Centuries of Social Life* [11]; Jordan's *From Rollo to Tom Sawyer* [12]; Kiefer's *American Children Through Their Books, 1700–1835,* [13]; and Thwaite's *From Primer to Pleasure* [14] better books to begin on. The characteristic they share in common is the connections made between the type of book being written and the social attitudes of the times.

As we read histories of children's literature, we should keep a file on books we will want to read or reread. It is not enough for a librarian to have only a childhood memory of loving or hating *Alice's Adventures in Wonderland, The Water Babies,* or even *Elsie Dinsmore.* Reading historical children's titles as an adult can and ought to provoke the response: "Did I ever really love this book?", or "Gee, I had good taste as a child."

The first step with older titles—particularly with the so-called classics—is to discover our own adult reactions to them. The second step is to evaluate the books in terms of their potential appeal to today's readers. There are many older books that appeal to an adult reader, but we must be aware constantly that there may be an enormous difference between an adult's reaction and a child's reaction to a book.

After reading a few books on the history of children's literature, we may discover that we are more interested in a particular type of book rather than the entire field. Children's book illustration is one such area that captures the enthusiasm of librarians.

Picture Books

There is a magic in a picture book that is surpassed only by the magic of a poem. Both picture book and poem make a small segment of the truth of human existence come alive for us.

It is of no consequence to children of the 1970s that *Millions of Cats* (1928) is half a century old or that many of the works of Robert McCloskey and Dr. Seuss are older than their parents. The on-going attraction of good picture books naturally stimulates critical attention, which has produced an impressive number of books about illustration and illustrators.

Here again, we will want to begin historically. Some familiarity with Randolph Caldecott, Kate Greenaway, Leslie Brooke, Howard Pyle, and Arthur Ransome, to mention just a few of the men and women who have contributed much to children's book illustration, is essential.

Perhaps because I know less about art than about literature, I find the general surveys of the current state of picture-book illustration very useful. There are three books on illustration that I particularly enjoy. Donnarae MacCann and Olga Richard's *The Child's First Books,* [15] *Picture-Book World* [16] by Bettina Hürlimann, and *Picture Books for Children,* [17] edited by Patricia Cianciolo in conjunction with the Picture Book Committee of the National Council of Teachers of English.

The MacCann-Richard volume pays as much attention to the text of picture books as it does to their illustration, which is a strong point in its favor. The authors are knowledgeable and perceptive critics. Especially important is their chapter on illustrators as writers since many illustrators do now write their own texts.

Hürlimann's *Picture-Book World* is just that, a look at picture books from twenty-four countries. It is testimony to the truth of Paul Hazard's words: "Every country gives and every country receives—innumerable are the exchanges—and so it comes about that in our first impressionable years the universal republic of childhood is born." [18] Profusely illustrated and offering us the opportunity to see the work of some illustrators whose books are not easily available outside their native country, *Picture-Book*

146

World is essential for librarians working in libraries without a good collection of books from abroad.

Picture Books for Children is basically an annotated bibliography, but certainly one of the most attractive ever published. It is divided into four major sections: "Me and My Family," "Other People," "The World I Live In," and "The Imaginative World." An important feature of the book is that it includes nonfiction and poetry as well as the traditional fictional picture book. While it is more useful as a buying guide than as a critical commentary on picture books, anyone who is familiar with the books recommended will have a very fine background upon which to build.

SPECIALIZING

After acquiring a reasonable general knowledge, it is possible to identify hundreds of areas for specialization: early nineteenth-century children's literature, folklore, storytelling, visual literacy, illustrations, biography, etc. What is important is the process of specialization, not the subject.

One benefit of becoming a specialist is that it teaches us that things are never as simple as they appear. This is a good lesson to learn. It keeps us alert to flaws of reasoning in articles or books we read. It teaches us that people who make too many unqualified statements, who see the world in either-or terms, are not to be granted too much credibility.

Children's librarianship—whether on the general or specialist level—offers the conscientious adult a multitude of opportunities for personal growth. Only self-imposed limitations keep us from enjoying the best of all combinations: intellectually curious children and intellectually challenging materials.

NOTES FOR CHAPTER 10

1. *Top of the News*, American Library Association, 50 East Huron Street, Chicago, IL 60611.
2. *Children's Literature in Education*, APS Publications, Inc., 150 Fifth Avenue, New York, NY 10011.
3. *Language Arts*, National Council of Teachers of English. 1111 Kenyon Road, Urbana, IL 61820.
4. *English Journal*, NCTE, address same as above.
5. *Library Journal*, R. R. Bowker, 1180 Avenue of the Americas, New York, NY 10036.
6. *School Library Journal*, Bowker, address same as above.
7. *Wilson Library Bulletin*, 950 University Avenue, Bronx, NY 10452.
8. *Horn Book*, 585 Boylston Street, Boston, MA 02116.
9. Virginia Haviland, *Children's Literature; A Guide to Reference Sources*, Washington, D.C.: Library of Congress, 1966. First Supplement, 1972.
10. Cornelia Meigs, *et al.*, *A Critical History of Children's Literature*, rev. ed., New York: Macmillan, 1968.
11. F. J. H. Darton, *Children's Books in England: Five Centuries of Social Life*, 2nd ed., London: Cambridge Univ. Press, 1958.
12. Alice M. Jordan, *From Rollo to Tom Sawyer*, Boston: Horn Book, 1948.
13. Monica Kiefer, *American Children Through Their Books, 1700–1835*, Philadelphia: Univ. of Pa. Press, 1948.
14. Mary Thwaite, *From Primer to Pleasure*, 2nd ed., London: The Library Association, 1972.
15. Donnarae MacCann and Olga Richard, *The Child's First Books; A Critical Study of Pictures and Texts*, New York: H. W. Wilson, 1973.
16. Bettina Hürlimann, *Picture-Book World*, translated and edited by Brian W. Alderson, Cleveland: World Pub, 1969.
17. *Picture Books for Children*, edited by Patricia Jean Cianciolo, Chicago: American Library Association, 1973.
18. Paul Hazard, *Books, Children and Men*, translated by Marguerite Mitchell, 4th ed. Boston: Horn Book, 1960, p. 146.

APPENDIX A

1972 CSD STATEMENT ON REEVALUATION OF CHILDREN'S MATERIALS

Librarians have a two-fold obligation in service to the child:

1. To build and maintain a collection of materials which provides information on the entire spectrum of human knowledge, experience, and opinion.
2. To actively introduce to the child those titles which will enable him to develop a free spirit, an inquiring mind, and an ever-widening knowledge of the culture in which he lives.

Most books, whether intentionally or not, reflect the social climate and conscience of the era in which they were written, and their readers at the time of publication accept this reflection without noticing it. But social climate, and conscience and man's state of knowledge are constantly changing. Therefore librarians must continuously reevaluate their old "standard" titles in the light of current progress.

In the process of reevaluation, it may be found that a highly respected title presents hitherto unnoticed misinformation or stereotypes in character, plot, dialog, and illustrations that are inaccurate in the light of current knowledge or beliefs and are demeaning to some segment of our society. When it is clear from the context in which these are presented that they reflect a past era, this title may still serve a useful role in a library collection. We cannot erase the past, and indeed it would be a disservice to the child to do so—to pretend that discrimination, prejudice, and misinformation never existed. But when it is not clear from the context that the book belongs to a past era, when it apparently fosters for the present day concepts which are now deemed false or degrading, then, despite the title's prestige, the librarian should question the validity of its continued inclusion in the library collection.

In making his decision, the librarian has a professional obligation to set aside personal likes and dislikes: to consider the "objectionable" material within the context of the book as a whole and then to consider the book as a whole with objectivity and respect for all opinions. Only *after* such consideration can he reach one of the three conclusions:

1. That other qualities in the book are so fine they outweigh the new-found flaws and that therefore he will continue to promote it while at the same time alerting the reader to its faults.
2. That the book should remain in the collection to fill specific title requests but should no longer be actively promoted.
3. That in comparison with contemporary thought and social climate the title is so misleading, or superseded in coverage and quality, that it is no longer valid library material and should be permanently discarded.

APPENDIX B

CSD STATEMENT ON REEVALUATION OF LIBRARY
MATERIALS—REVISED 1973

Librarians must espouse critical standards in selection and reevaluation of library materials. It is incumbent on the librarian working with children to be aware that the child lacks the breadth of experience of the adult and that librarians have a twofold obligation in service to the child:

1. To build and maintain collections of materials which provide information on the entire spectrum of human knowledge, experience, and opinion.

2. To introduce to the child those titles which will enable him to develop with a free spirit, an inquiring mind, and an ever widening knowledge of the world in which he lives.

Because most materials reflect the social climate of the era in which they are produced, it is often difficult to evaluate some aspects of a work at the time of purchase. But social climate and man's state of knowledge are constantly changing and librarians should therefore continuously reevaluate their old materials in the light of growing knowledge and broadening perspectives. In the process of reevaluation it may be found that an old title is still fresh and pertinent, or even, that it was produced ahead of its time and now has a new relevance. It may, on the other hand, no longer serve a useful role in the collections. It may have been superseded by better books.

In making his decision, the librarian has a professional obligation to set aside personal likes and dislikes, to avoid labeling materials, to consider the strengths and weaknesses of each title, and to consider the material as a whole with objectivity and respect for all opinions. Only after such consideration can he reach a decision as to whether the title is superseded in coverage and quality, and should be discarded, or should be kept in the collection.

The Board of Directors of the Children's Services Division, American Library Association, supports the Library Bill of Right and Free Access to Libraries for Minors. Reevaluation is a positive approach.

APPENDIX C

CSD INTELLECTUAL FREEDOM COMMITTEE:
STATEMENT TO THE CSD BOARD JANUARY 21, 1976

At ALA's Annual Conference in Chicago in June 1972, the ALA-Children's Book Council Joint Committee sponsored a preconference on changing criteria and the role of reevaluation in children's book selection. [1] *Library Journal* and *School Library Journal* published the papers read at the preconference, [2] but the small group discussions were deliberately not recorded and not summarized; no proceedings were published, and no conclusions were stated. However, at that same conference, the CSD Board endorsed the ALA Intellectual Freedom Committee's statement on "Free Access to Libraries for Minors" and also issued a CSD "Statement on Reevaluation of Children's Materials." [3, 4] On July 24, 1972, the chairperson of ALA's Intellectual Freedom Committee wrote a letter to the president of the Children's Services Division expressing concern that the CSD Statement seriously conflicted with longstanding and recent intellectual freedom policies of ALA. [5] He articulated seven areas of conflict:

1. "The thesis that misinformation or inaccurate representation may render certain works unacceptable for library collections" conflicts with Article II of the *Library Bill of Rights* [6] which states "no library materials should be proscribed or removed from libraries because of partisan or doctrinal disapproval." [7]

2. To indicate that "a librarian may remove material 'that in comparison with contemporary thought and social climate . . . is so misleading, or superseded in coverage and quality, that it is no longer valid library material . . . ' " violates Article I of the *Library Bill of Rights* which states "in no case should library materials be excluded because of the race or nationality or the social, political, or religious views of the authors." [8]

3. The statement "that a librarian might conclude 'that other qualities in the material are so fine they outweigh the new found flaws and that therefore he will continue to promote it while at the same time alerting the user to its fault' " conflicts with the ALA "State-

ment on Labeling"[9] which prohibits "the practice of describing or designating certain library materials by affixing a prejudicial label to them or segregating them by a prejudicial system so as to predispose readers against the materials."[10]

4. "The CSD Statement also conflicts with several parts of the 'Freedom to Read Statement' . . . and the 'Intellectual Freedom Statement' "[11, 12] (ALA policy statements), both of which endorse provision of the "widest diversity of views and expressions . . . including those which are strange, unorthodox or unpopular."[13]

5. "Not in . . . text—but certainly in its application—the CSD Statement also conflicts with the policy entitled 'Free Access to Libraries for Minors'[14] which holds that 'it is the parent—and only the parent — who may restrict his children —and only *his* children—from access to library materials and services.' Exclusion of materials, through the 'reevaluation' process as described in the CSD Statement, surely restricts access to material by eliminating it completely."[15]

6 and 7. "The CSD Statement conflicts with two of [the ALA Intellectual Freedom Committee's] . . . advisory statements: 'Advisory Statement on the Reevaluation of Library Materials'[16] . . . and 'Advisory Statement on Racism, Sexism and Other "Isms" in Library Materials.' "[17] (Both of these statements have since been adopted as official ALA policy.)[18]

The ALA Intellectual Freedom Committee's letter to the president of CSD engendered a great deal of debate. The issue was reported in the media;[19] *Top of the News* carried a statement that solicited opinions from CSD members,[20] and a joint meeting of the ALA Intellectual Freedom Committee and the CSD Board was scheduled for Midwinter 1973 in Washington, D.C.

The opinions expressed by CSD membership[21] ranged all the way from the statement of the children's librarian who contended that the CSD Statement was "ambiguous and imprecise" and failed to grapple with issues such as "the validity of the diverse criteria by which adults evaluate materials for children; the question of children's access to published materials and the related question of who determines what is published for children, and the role and responsibility of the children's librarian in matters of selection, acquisition and promotion of materials"[22] to the statement of the children's librarian who maintained that the CSD Statement was "supportive of what children's librarians consider to be a sound philosophy of continuous critical evaluation" and "supportive of selection standards and in accord with Intellectual Freedom policies in letter and spirit; i.e., supportive of and encouraging of

153

decisions to retain titles so long as they are useful, pertinent, and in demand." [23]

At the joint meeting at Midwinter 1973, discussion was limited to "clarification of the respective positions of CSD and the Intellectual Freedom Committee with the hope of resolving apparent differences." [24] No action was taken. CSD presented a draft of a new statement for discussion. Members of the Intellectual Freedom Committee proposed several changes; for example, "to build and maintain a collection of materials" was changed to "to build and maintain collections of materials." The sentence, "It may, on the other hand, be outmoded or factually inaccurate, no longer serving a useful role . . ." was changed to "It may, on the other hand, no longer serve a useful role in the collection." A member of the Intellectual Freedom Committee suggested that the CSD Statement include an affirmation of the *Library Bill of Rights* and "Free Access to Libraries for Minors." [25] These suggestions were accepted by the CSD Board, and the CSD Board issued a revised "Statement on Reevaluation of Library Materials for Children's Collections." [26]

It must be noted that the ALA Intellectual Freedom Committee did not endorse the revised statement. The minutes of the Intellectual Freedom Committee's meeting on January 29, 1973, second session, contain this note: "Mr. Eshelman, guest, asked about the committee's view of the IFC/CSD joint meeting. Mr. Darling replied that although apparently there was no meeting of the minds, the revised statement on 'Reevaluation of Children's Collections' did not contain the objectionable passages of the former. He added that obvious philosophical differences remained, and that he did not know what the committee could do to remove them." [27]

Discussion and debate on the question of reevaluation have continued. A number of important articles on the topic have appeared in issues of *LJ/SLJ*—articles on racism, sexism, selection criteria, and the question of whether or not the children's librarian does stand *in loco parentis*. Many of these have been reprinted in the Bowker anthology *Issues in Children's Book Selection.* [28]

Shortly after the 1973 Midwinter Meeting, *Wilson Library Bulletin* published an "Overdue" column by Helen Kreigh who pointed to such grim realities as the case of the school librarians whose suburban system had to resubmit a school bond issue seven times before it was approved by voters at the price of censorship of curricular and library materials. Helen Kreigh urged that librarians "not dissipate . . . energies and resources on family squabbles over semantics while flames lick unnoticed at the drawbridge and walls of one of the smallest bastions there still is." She states that she understands the intention (of the CSD Statement) and "will not be misled in any important way" regarding her support and practice of intellectual freedom. [29]

However, letters and articles that have appeared in the media, [30] letters received by the Intellectual Freedom Committee of CSD and conversations that the CSD Intellectual Freedom Committee members have had with many librarians indicate that librarians *have* been misled and that confusion persists concerning the application of the CSD "Statement on Reevaluation of Library Materials for Children's Collections."

An editorial in *SLJ*, April 1975, brings the issues sharply into focus, stating that ALA Council-approved interpretations of the *Library Bill of Rights* including "Free Access to Libraries for Minors—1972," "Sexism, Racism and Other 'Isms' in Library Materials—1973," and "Reevaluating Library Collections— 1973" are at "wide variance from statements adopted by ALA's three youth services divisions" (CSD, YASD, and AASL). ALA policies "overlook the fact that public and school libraries must operate within the local, state and federal laws governing minors and [they] ignore the idea of adult responsibility in relation to the welfare of minors held by librarians as well as [by] other professional service groups, such as teachers, psychologists and guidance counselors." [31]

The editorial states further that AASL is revising the 1969 *School Library Bill of Rights for School Media Center Programs* and that the "first draft of the revision retains a paragraph that restates the judgmental responsibilities in school library materials selection. . . ." [32]

The editorial states further that a 1972 YASD statement on accessibility says "Adults (parents, teachers, librarians) should help provide a climate in which development of disciplined freedom in thought and conscience can take place." If "discipline" connotes "to bring a group under control, to impose order upon, training that corrects, molds or perfects . . . the term appears to call for the interposition of adult authority and judgment between YA's and their full access to library materials." [33]

Finally, the *SLJ* editorial notes that the CSD "Statement on Reevaluation" begins with a "sharp reminder" that "it is *incumbent* on the librarian working with children to be aware that the child lacks the breadth of experience of the adult." [34]

The editorial concludes that the issues "are still crucial, increasingly divisive and overdue for discussion and resolution between ALA Council and its youth services divisions." [35]

The admonishment in the CSD Statement to remember that "the child lacks the breadth of experience of the adult" [36] seems to lend credence to the arguments of the librarian, in a letter to the CSD Intellectual Freedom Committee, that it would be irresponsible and damaging to the child to give a black or white child *Amos Fortune, Free Man* [37] or *The Voyages of Dr. Dolittle,* [38] because of racial slurs and misinformation in both books, unless the child was also given extensive background in such subjects as black history and culture, European colonialism, the economics underlying slavery in America, racist behavior patterns, etc. The letter calls attention to research on the adverse effects of racism upon the mental health of children and takes the position that racist books reinforce the teachings of a racist society and should therefore be removed from the shelves. The letter endorses the CSD "Statement on Reevaluation." [39]

Another letter calls the CSD Statement "vague" and "pernicious"—a doctrine of self-imposed censorship which "could easily be used to justify the withdrawal of many books of interest to children because they are not in agreement with an individual librarian's principles." [40]

Another letter to the CSD Intellectual Freedom Committee does not state clearly whether the writer recommends that CSD retain or rescind the "Statement on Reevaluation," but it documents confusion. The writer says, "many librarians who deal with children do not know and/or understand the 'language' of education or library science. There is a need to oversimplify so that there can be *no misunderstanding* and *no margin left for misinterpretation.*" [41]

The CSD Intellectual Freedom Committee submits that the CSD "Statement on Reevaluation" leaves a wide margin for misinterpretation and actually encourages questionable weeding practices. The sentence in the CSD Statement that says "But social climate and man's state of knowledge are constantly changing and librarians should therefore continuously reevaluate their old materials in the light of growing knowledge and broadening perspectives" [42] appears to be based on the belief that, at any given time, it is possible to determine exactly what knowledge and values are the correct knowledge and values; that this correct knowledge and these correct values should be incorporated into all materials approved for children's use; that society as a whole agrees on the knowledge and values to be transmitted to children; and that incorporating this knowledge and these values into materials for children will ensure that children *will acquire* the correct knowledge and will internalize the correct values (if they use the materials). By implication, the CSD "Statement on Reevaluation of Library Materials for Children's Collections" seems to be saying that to expose children to misinformation, or to communicate false values, will cause irretrievable damage and irreversible harm.

This is the same position subscribed to by nineteenth-century moralists, authors, teachers, critics, parents, and librarians who steadfastly maintained that all books for children must "mold moral fiber," "shape virtuous character," and encourage "dedication to good and useful things. . . ." [43] "Proper" subjects for fiction included "fidelity to nature; to moral truth; regard to the public good; . . . endearing scenes of domestic life; generosity and gratitude; [and] filial, parental and fraternal love." [44]

Anne Scott MacLeod's book *A Moral Tale* (Archon, 1975) reminds us that subjects considered "appropriate" for children's books have varied throughout history. Some issues that have been largely ignored in the last fifty years in books for children were dealt with in gory detail in the middle of the nineteenth century: death, poverty, drunkenness, the horrors of war. But writers for children of the same period avoided the question of slavery; anti-slavery sentiment was too hot a topic for children's books. MacLeod goes on to tell us that while materialism was decried in popular literature of the nineteenth century and the literature suffused with the ideal of Christian morality, that ideal was "far removed from the reality of getting and grasping in the Jacksonian era." [45]

In nineteenth-century fiction for children, selfishness is condemned as a primary fault, and ambition (or restless striving) is deplored in apparent reaction against the competitiveness, turbulence, individualism, and industrial development of Jacksonian America, but at the same time the virtues of industry and hard work are always extolled and always rewarded. And the most visible occupations in children's fiction of the period are those connected with business and commerce. There are almost no tradesmen, factory workers, lawyers, doctors, or farmers —evidence that the writers unconsciously accepted many of the social and economic values of their societies. [46]

One hundred and fifty years ago, and still today, the crux of the matter—the really sensitive issue—is the question of what criteria we use in the selection and evaluation of children's materials.

In the absence of a clear policy statement on selection and evaluation, it is most difficult, perhaps impossible, to frame a clear, unambiguous statement on reevaluation.

The CSD "Statement on Reevaluation of Library Materials for Children's Collections" insists that "Librarians must espouse *critical standards* in selection and reevaluation of library materials";[47] but the critical standards are not defined. Statements of criteria are scattered in bits and pieces throughout the literature on library services to children. *Standards for Children's Services in Public Libraries* talks about "the effectiveness and quality of resources."[48] Lillian Smith speaks about "books of honesty, integrity and vision";[49] Paul Hazard asks for "books that contain a profound morality" but also "books which respect . . . play."[50]

Greatly oversimplified, it can be said that in the nineteenth century the chief critical standard was the correct moral stance of the material. In the twentieth century the chief critical standard, endorsed by CSD, has been the quality of literary excellence. At the three-quarter mark in the twentieth century we seem to be returning to the position that children's books are best measured by the appropriateness of their content, in terms of the extent to which they communicate correct social attitudes and values.

In the nineteenth century, perhaps—*perhaps*—U.S. society *as a whole* agreed on *one* interpretation of what constituted *correct* moral attitudes and behavior. And while there can be—and usually *is*—debate about the application of literary criteria, the criteria themselves are fairly standard. However, in our diverse, multicultural, multiracial, multi-ethnic, contemporary society, how can we suppose we can easily agree on the values to be transmitted to children? (Disregarding the separate issue of whether or not children's books actually play a significant role in the transmission of values.)

Here are examples of some isolated criteria for juvenile selection: Eakin says, "Family and age-mate relationships should be sound, healthy ones."[51] How do such titles as *Mom, the Wolf Man and Me; Grover; My Brother Stevie; Good Boy, Bad Boy;* and *How Many Miles to Babylon* measure up to these criteria?[52-56]

In 1964 Arbuthnot asked, in a discussion of style: "does [the book] add to the children's zest for living, their feeling that life is good?"[57] How do titles such as *The Little Fishes, Dorp Dead, The Planet of Junior Brown,* and *Edgar Allen* meet these criteria?[58-61] In 1972 Sutherland, revising Arbuthnot, tells us that style is almost impossible to define.[62]

So-called new criteria have been announced by feminists and groups that represent blacks, Spanish-speaking peoples, and American Indians. The ALA/ASD Subcommittee on Indian Material wanted us to ask "does the material present both sides of the event, issue, problem or other concern?" [63] If we apply that standard strictly, we must toss out Laura Ingalls Wilder's "Little House" books. [64] Are we ready and willing to discard Wilder?

Do we agree with the Council on Interracial Books that the only valid books about blacks and other minority groups are those written by members of the minority groups? [65] Do we endorse the statement of the librarian who publicly regretted that *The Cay*, by Taylor, received the Addams Award? [66]

The phrase in the CSD Statement "constantly changing social climate" sounds perilously like the Supreme Court's phrase "contemporary community standards." [67] We deplore the application of "contemporary community standards" in obscenity cases. Do we really want to encourage the application of these criteria to selection and evaluation of children's materials?

In some communities (black as well as white) *Little Black Sambo* is acceptable; in others, not. [68] In some communities *Charlie and the Chocolate Factory* is regarded as a very funny book, a very apt and cutting satire on American values and behavior; in other communities it is considered a racist tract. [69] The Council on Interracial Books gave *The Soul Brothers and Sister Lou* [70] its first Award. The book was embraced by the black community—and why not? It was one of the first contemporary black teen novels set in the ghetto. But some members of the white community objected to the stereotyped portrayal of the white policeman.

And how do we evaluate *Show Me!?* [71] Some children's librarians consider it pornography. A Superior Court Judge in Massachusetts refused to declare the book legally obscene, maintaining it has social value despite its appeal to prurient interest. [72] Melinda Schroeder wrote a review in *Booklegger* which points out that the book promulgates old myths: people should have sex only if in love; the ultimate aim of sex is marriage and children; every child must relate to one mother figure for healthy development; the father's role is peripheral; boys get more out of sex than girls; women automatically reach orgasm through intercourse. The reviewer calls the last statement "cruel misinformation that can only lead to unnecessary deprivation, suffering and guilt on the part of the larger portion of the female population." Still, she recommends the book for library purchase as going far beyond traditional children's sex-education books. She feels it deserves a place in our collections as "one of those books that's better than nothing till something better comes along." [73]

What do we say to the Catholic parents who, in the light of the re-

159

cent Vatican document that states that masturbation is an intrinsically disordered act, may argue that all of our materials on sex education that maintain masturbation is part of the normal process of maturation and development are communicating misinformation and false values to Catholic children?[74]

How do we answer the white and black suburban parents who object to the use of "black English" in John Steptoe's books?[75]

What do we say to the social workers and librarians who would have us remove titles such as *Take Wing,*[76] *Don't Take Teddy,*[77] and *Hey, Dummy*[78] because these books emphasize the *burdens* that the attitudes of our society place upon the siblings and friends of retarded persons and point out the ways in which retarded people appear frightening, awkward, messy and different from so-called normal people?[79] While it is true that these books may not reinforce a positive attitude toward mainstreaming and integration, they represent one aspect of the reality of the contemporary situation. And children must learn to confront and control their instinctive feelings of distress and repugnance when they encounter a grossly deformed or disfigured person. A collection of books that portray retarded people only in warm, loving family-peer group situations would contradict children's experience of reality and not necessarily improve their treatment of the retarded, any more than books that preach brotherhood make children more brotherly or more understanding, or books that extol piety make children more devout.

There is no conclusive research that tells us how media influence behavior or the development of values.

Admittedly, we live in a racist and sexist society; a violent society; a society infested with venereal disease but constrained by an assortment of sexual taboos that inhibit adults from giving intelligent guidance and information to young people; a society in which handicapped people are excluded and invisible victims of discrimination. Admittedly, books in our children's collections reflect racist, sexist, and puritanical attitudes. But removing these books from our shelves will not eradicate racism, sexism, or puritanism. Should we not devote our energies to broadening our collections to include materials that will counteract stubborn prejudice and bias—materials produced by alternative, third-world, small, radical, and feminist presses?

Even Bradford Chambers (director of the Council on Interracial Books for Children), in March 1975, at a New York Women's National Book Association meeting, "denied that the Council on Interracial Books had ever called for return or removal of past awards, the censorship of children's books, or their removal from library collections." [80]

CSD cannot, with logic, endorse ALA's *Library Bill of Rights* and ALA's statement on "Free Access to Libraries for Minors" and, at the same time, maintain that as adults we have a responsibility and a right to make value judgments about which materials are "appropriate" to give to children.

Notice that I said which materials are "appropriate," not which materials possess "literary quality." There is a difference between criticism and materials selection. All too often we blur the distinction. We needn't abandon our efforts to identify creative, imaginative, substantive materials and to communicate our enthusiasm for those materials to children. But, if we are honest, we will acknowledge that our collections contain many titles that have no literary merit, no aesthetic appeal, but are useful and needed or wanted by the children and parents who use our libraries. Children's librarians are not, and cannot be, only literature specialists. We are reference librarians, information specialists and idea persons to children, and resource people to adults concerned with children. We need broad collections to answer diverse needs. I urge that you reread Sara Fenwick's positive statement on reevaluation in the January-April 1972 issue of the *Calendar* of the Children's Book Council in which she asks librarians to seek out and reconsider certain titles we have not added to our collections, books that we rejected the first time around. [81]

Last night I received a letter from Pat Finley (CSD/IFC chairperson, 1972–74) containing a copy of another letter concerning the CSD "Statement on Reevaluation." The letter says, in part, the "statement on reevaluation . . . was nothing more than a plea for guidelines for . . . careful thoughtful selection . . . to assure [children] finding books that will stimulate thought, sensitivity and imagination rather than books that could create or feed prejudice or racism." [82]

Unfortunately, the CSD "Statement on Reevaluation of Library Materials for Children's Collections" does not provide any such guidelines. One librarian of my acquaintance has used the Statement to justify both her removal of Wilder books and her purchase of "Nancy Drew." I doubt that this is what the framers of the CSD Statement had in mind.

The ALA Council has adopted a series of policy statements which provide librarians with a substantial defense against censorship. Unless and until we can make, justify, support, and defend a special case for treating children and children's collections in a wholly different manner (and, in a climate of growing concern about the legal rights of chil-

161

dren, this may be impossible to do), let us accept ALA policy as CSD policy.

To dispel confusion and to protect librarians and library collections from censors, the members of the CSD Intellectual Freedom Committee respectfully recommend that the CSD Board rescind the 1973 CSD "Statement on Reevaluation of Library Materials for Children's Collections."

APPENDIX C

REFERENCES

1."Children's Books in a Changing World: New Criteria for Evaluation. A One-Day Preconference Institute Sponsored by the American Library Association—Children's Book Council Joint Committee," Conrad Hilton Hotel, Chicago, June 24, 1972.

2. "Preconference Institute on Children's Books and the Changing World: New Criteria for Evaluation, 1972, Chicago." [Papers]. *Library Journal* 97:3421-39 (Oct. 15, 1972); *School Library Journal* 19:79-97 (Oct. 1972).

3. American Library Association, "Free Access to Libraries for Minors: An Interpretation of the 'Library Bill of Rights,' " approved June 30, 1972, by the ALA Council, in *Intellectual Freedom Manual*, compiled by the Office for Intellectual Freedom of the American Library Association (Chicago: American Library Assn., 1974), Part I, p.16-17.

4. ALA Children's Services Division, "Statement on Reevaluation of Children's Materials," adopted by the CSD Board, June 28, 1972, text in *Top of the News* 29:15-16 (Nov. 1972).

5. Richard L. Darling, Letter to Anne Izard, July 24, 1972.

6. American Library Association, "Library Bill of Rights," adopted June 18, 1948, amended Feb. 2, 1961, and June 27, 1967, by the ALA Council, in *Intellectual Freedom Manual*, Part I, p.11.

7. Richard L. Darling, Letter to Anne Izard, July 24, 1972.

8. Ibid.

9. American Library Association, "Statement on Labeling," adopted July 13, 1951, amended June 25, 1971, by the ALA Council, in *Intellectual Freedom Manual*, Part I, p.22.

10. Richard L. Darling, Letter to Anne Izard, July 24, 1972.

11. American Library Association, "The Freedom To Read," issued in May 1953, by the Westchester Conference of the American Library Association and the American Book Publishers Council, since 1970 the Association of American Publishers, adopted June 25, 1953, revised Jan. 28, 1972, by the ALA Council, in *Intellectual Freedom Manual*, Part II, p.14-19.

12. American Library Association, "Intellectual Freedom Statement: An Interpretation of the 'Library Bill of Rights,' " adopted June 25, 1971, by the ALA Council, in *Intellectual Freedom Manual*, Part I, p.47-50.

13. Richard L. Darling, Letter to Anne Izard, July 24, 1972.

14. American Library Association, "Free Access to Libraries for Minors."

15. Richard L. Darling, Letter to Anne Izard, July 24, 1972.

16. American Library Association, "Reevaluating Library Collections: An Interpretation of the 'Library Bill of Rights,' " adopted Feb. 2, 1973, by the ALA Council, in *Intellectual Freedom Manual*, Part I, p.31.

17. American Library Association, "Sexism, Racism, and Other-Isms in Library Materials: An Interpretation of the 'Library Bill of Rights,' " adopted Feb. 2, 1973, by the ALA Council, in *Intellectual Freedom Manual*, Part I, p.27-29.

APPENDIX C

18. Richard L. Darling, Letter to Anne Izard, July 24, 1972.

19. Arthur Plotnik, "Title Should Be Permanently Discarded: Statement on Reevaluation of Children's Materials Adopted by the Children's Services Division Board," *Wilson Library Bulletin* 47:122 (Oct. 1972); "IFC Warns CSD on Reevaluation Statement," *Library Journal* 97:3751–52 (Nov. 15, 1972); *School Library Journal* 19:13–14 (Nov. 1972); "CSD Withdraws Materials Statement," American Libraries 3:1159 (Dec. 1972).

20. "Children's Services Division of the American Library Association Adopted a Statement on Reevaluation of Children's Materials," *Top of the News* 29:15 (Nov. 1972).

21. See articles and letters indexed in *Library Literature 1973* (New York: Wilson, 1974) under "Children's Literature: Evaluation."

22. Diane Farrell, Informal Comments to the Board of the New England Round Table of Children's Librarians, Dec. 4, 1972, and Letter to Anne Izard, Jan. 23, 1973.

23. Mary Jane Anderson, "Editor's Note: An Open Letter to the President of CSD," *Top of the News* 29:115–16 (Jan. 1973).

24. ALA Intellectual Freedom Committee, "Minutes," First Session, Jan. 29, 1973, p.4; ALA Intellectual Freedom Committee—ALA Children's Services Division, "Minutes of a Joint Meeting," Jan. 29, 1973, p.1.

25. ALA Intellectual Freedom Committee—ALA Children's Services Division, "Minutes of a Joint Meeting," Jan. 29, 1973, p.2.

26. ALA Children's Services Division, "Statement on Reevaluation of Library Materials for Children's Collections," adopted by the CSD Board, Jan. 29, 1973, text in *Top of the News* 29:190–91 (April 1973).

27. ALA Intellectual Freedom Committee, "Minutes," Third Session, Jan. 30, 1973, p.13.

28. *Issues in Children's Book Selection: A School Library Journal/Library Journal Anthology* (New York: Bowker, 1973).

29. Helen Kreigh, "Overdue: Unaccustomed As I Am to Viewing From the Fence--," *Wilson Library Bulletin* 47:527 (Feb. 1973).

30. Betsy Rush, "Weeding vs. Censorship: Treading a Fine Line," *Library Journal* 99: 3032–33 (Nov. 15, 1974); *School Library Journal* 21:42–43 (Nov. 1974); Pat Finley, "Who Misunderstood?" [letter] *School Library Journal* 21:3 (Feb. 1975); Comment [letters] *School Library Journal* 21:3 (May 1975), 22:2 (Sept. 1975); "Censorship and Racism: A Dilemma for Librarians"; Wayne Kabak, "Librarians Wrestle with Racism, Sexism," *Interracial Books for Children Bulletin* 6, No. 3 and 4:1 (1975), "The Slave Dancer: Critiques of this Year's Newbery Award-Winner," *Interracial Books for Children Bulletin* 5, No. 5:4–5 (1974); see also articles and letters indexed in *Library Literature 1973, 1974,* and *1975* under "Children's Literature: Evaluation," and articles and letters in issues of *Interracial Books for Children Bulletin* 1973–1975.

31. Lillian N. Gerhardt, "SLJ/Editorial: Freedom From Cant—Now!" *School Library Journal* 21:7 (April 1975).

32. Ibid.

33. Ibid.

34. Ibid.

35. Ibid.

36. ALA Children's Services Division, "Statement on Reevaluation of Library Materials for Children's Collections."

37. Elizabeth Yates, *Amos Fortune, Free Man* (New York: Dutton, 1950).

38. Hugh Lofting, *The Voyages of Dr. Doolittle* (Philadelphia, Lippincott, 1922).

39. Donnarae MacCann, Letter to CSD/IFC chairperson, Nov. 18, 1975.

40. Margaret Sheeran, Letter to CSD/IFC chairperson, Nov. 14, 1975.

41. Gloria Jay Pickens, Letter to CSD/IFC chairperson, Nov. 15, 1975.

42. ALA Children's Services Division, "Statement on Reevaluation of Library Materials for Children's Collections."

43. Anne Scott MacLeod, A Moral Tale: Children's Fiction and American Culture, 1820–1860 (Hamden, Conn.: Archon, 1975), p.25.

44. Ibid., p.27.

45. Ibid., p.27–28; 56–68; 104–17.

46. Ibid., p.83–89; 96–98; 147–50.

47. ALA Children's Services Division, "Statement on Reevaluation of Library Materials for Children's Collections."

48. ALA Public Library Association, Standards for Children's Services in Public Libraries (Chicago: American Library Assn., 1964), p.22.

49. Lillian Smith, The Unreluctant Years: A Critical Approach to Children's Literature (Chicago: Amercian Library Assn., 1953), p.14.

50. Paul Hazard, Books, Children and Men (Boston: Horn Book, 1944), p.42–45.

51. Mary K. Eakin, Good Books for Children (3d ed.; Chicago: Univ. of Chicago Press, 1966), p.xii.

52. Norma Klein, Mom, the Wolf Man and Me (New York: Pantheon, 1973).

53. Vera Cleaver and Bill Cleaver, Grover (Philadelphia: Lippincott, 1970).

54. Eleanor Clymer, My Brother Stevie (New York: Holt, 1967).

55. Marie Hall Ets, Good Boy, Bad Boy (New York: Crowell, 1967).

56. Paula Fox, How Many Miles to Babylon? (New York: White, 1967).

57. May Hill Arbuthnot, Children and Books, 3d ed. (Chicago: Scott, Foresman, 1964), p.19.

58. Erik Haugaard, The Little Fishes (Boston: Houghton, 1967).

59. Julia Cunningham, Dorp Dead (New York: Pantheon, 1965).

60. Virginia Hamilton, The Planet of Junior Brown (New York: Macmillan, 1971).

61. John Neufeld, Edgar Allan (New York: Phillips, 1968).

62. Zena Sutherland and May Hill Arbuthnot, Children and Books, 4th ed. (Chicago: Scott, Foresman, 1972).

63. ALA Adult Services Division Subcommittee on Indian Material, "Guidelines for the Evaluation of Indian Materials for Adults," ASD Newsletter 8, no. 3 (Spring 1971).

64. Laura Ingalls Wilder, Little House in the Big Woods (New York: Harper, 1953) and other titles in the series.

65. Albert V. Schwartz, " 'Sounder': A Black or a White Tale?" Interracial Books for Children Bulletin 3, no. 1 (1970); "100 Books about Puerto Ricans: A Study in Racism, Sexism and Colonialism," Interracial Books for Children Bulletin 4, no. 1 and 2 (1972).

66. Bertha Jenkinson, Statement made at press conference called by the Council on Interracial Books, Oct. 17, 1974, text in "Revoking 'The Cay' Award: The Establishment Cries Foul!" Interracial Books for Children Bulletin 6, no. 3 and 4 (1975) p.6–7.

67. Miller v California, June 21, 1973.

68. Helen Bannerman, Little Black Sambo (Philadelphia: Lippincott, 1923).

69. Roald Dahl, Charlie and the Chocolate Factory (New York: Knopf, 1964).

70. Kristin Hunter, The Soul Brothers and Sister Lou (New York: Scribner, 1968).

71. Helga Fleischhauer-Hardt, Show Me! A Picture Book of Sex for Children and Parents,

with photographs and captions by Will McBride (New York: St. Martin's, 1975).

72. "Book Wins Case," *Boston Globe* (Jan. 9, 1976).

73. Melinda Schroeder, "Kids and Libraries," review of Helga Fleischhauer-Hardt, *Show Me! A Picture Book of Sex for Children and Parents* (New York: St. Martin's, 1975), in *Booklegger* 11:32–34 (July/Aug. 1975).

74. Cardinal Franjo Seper, Prefect, and Father Jerome Hamer, O.P., Secretary, Sacred Congregation for the Doctrine of the Faith, "Declaration on Certain Questions Concerning Sexual Ethics," approved by Pope Paul VI, Nov. 7, 1975, published in Rome, Dec. 29, 1975, made public in the U.S. by the U.S. Catholic Conference-National Conference of Catholic Bishops, Jan. 15, 1976, English text in *The Pilot*, Special Supplement (Jan. 23, 1976).

75. John Steptoe, *Stevie* (New York: Harper, 1969); John Steptoe, *Uptown* (New York: Harper, 1970).

76. Jean Little, *Take Wing* (Boston: Little, 1968).

77. Babbis Friis-Bastaad, *Don't Take Teddy* (New York: Scribner, 1967).

78. Kin Platt, *Hey, Dummy* (Philadelphia: Chilton, 1971).

79. Ruth-Ann Rasbold and Bonnie Wilpon, "I Am Me and You Are You: An Annotated Bibliography of Books for Young People," in *Resource Materials for Serving Those With Special Needs* (Media Resource Center, Massachusetts Department of Mental Health, Box 158, Belmont, MA 02178, 1975).

80. Bradford Chambers, Statement made at a panel discussion sponsored by the New York Chapter of the Women's National Book Association, March 25, 1975, briefly summarized in "SLJ/Make Your Point," *School Library Journal* 21:39 (May 1975).

81. Sara Innes Fenwick, "Re-evaluation 1971, 1972 . . . ," *Calendar* 31, no. 1 (Jan.–April 1972).

82. Anne Izard, Letter to CSD/IFC chairperson, Jan. 12, 1976.

APPENDIX D

RESOLUTION ON RACISM & SEXISM AWARENESS

Adopted by the ALA Membership and Approved by Council in Meetings
Friday, July 23, 1976

WHEREAS, during the last 200 years the United States has failed to equalize the status of racial minorities and of women, and
WHEREAS, the American Library Association has professed belief in the principle of equality yet has failed to aggressively address the racism and sexism within its own professional province;
THEREFORE, BE IT RESOLVED, that the American Library Association actively commit its prestige and resources to a coordinated action program that will combat racism and sexism in the library profession and in library service by taking the following steps:

The ALA will survey library schools to determine the extent to which racism and sexism awareness training form a part of the curricula and urge that such training be added to the curricula in every library school where it is not now included.

The Library Administration-Personnel Administration Section will develop a model in-service program providing racism and sexism awareness training for library personnel.

The Public Library Association, the American Association of School Librarians, the Children's Services Division, the Young Adult Services Division, the Reference and Adult Services Division, and the Association of College and Research Libraries will be urged to develop a program to raise the awareness of library users to the pressing problem of racism and sexism.

The Resources and Technical Services Division will develop a coordinated plan for the reform of cataloging practices that now perpetuate racism and sexism.
BE IT FURTHER RESOLVED, that the President and Executive Board assess the extent of implementation of these steps and report on progress by the 1977 annual conference.

167

Bibliography

The following bibliography is selective, with as many points of view represented on a topic as could be found expressed. Some few entries are annotated when their titles would not indicate their content or when they were considered exceptionally important. To keep the bibliography up-to-date, readers are advised to consult *Library Literature Index* and *Social Sciences Index*.

CHILD DEVELOPMENT

Erikson, Erik H.

Erikson, Erik H. *Childhood and Society.* New York: Norton, 1950. (Also a Penguin pb.)
———— *Identity: Youth and Crisis.* New York: Norton, 1968.

Kohlberg, Lawrence (by and about)

Broderick, Dorothy M. "Moral Values and Children's Literature." In *Issues in Children's Book Selection.* New York: Bowker, 1973, pp. 35–9.
Duska, Ronald and Whelan, Mariellen. *Moral Development: A Guide to Piaget and Kohlberg.* New York: Paulist Press, 1975.
A Catholic/Christian view that offers important connections between religion and morality.
Galbraith, Ronald E. and Jones, T. R. *Moral Reasoning; A Teaching Handbook for Adapting Kohlberg to the Classroom.* Anoka, MN: Greenhaven Press, 1976.
Kohlberg, Lawrence. "The Child As a Moral Philosopher." *Psychology Today,* July 1968, pp. 25–30.
———— "The Development of Moral Character and Ideology." In Hoffman, M., ed. *Review of Child Psychology.* New York: Russell Sage Foundation, 1964, pp. 383–431.

―――― "Education for Justice." In Sizer, T., ed. *Moral Education*. Cambridge, MA: Harvard Univ. Press, 1970, pp. 57–83.

―――― "Moral Development and Identification." In Stevenson, H. W., ed. *Child Psychology 62nd Yearbook, National Social Studies Education, Part I.* Chicago: Univ. of Chicago Press, 1963, pp. 277–332.

―――― "Moral Education in the School." *School Review*, vol. 14, no. 1 (1966), pp. 1–30.

―――― "Stage and Sequence: The Cognitive-Developmental Approach to Socialization." In: Goslin, David, ed. *Handbook of Socialization Theory and Research*. New York: Rand McNally, 1969, pp. 347–480.

Naylor, Alice Phoebe. "Moral Education and Libraries." *Ohio Association of School Librarians Bulletin*, May 1976, pp. 30–4.

Piaget, Jean (by and about)

Evans, Richard I. *Jean Piaget: The Man and His Ideas*. Translated by Eleanor Duckworth. New York: Dutton, 1973.

Phillips, John L. *The Origins of Intellect: Piaget's Theory*. San Francisco: Freeman, 1969.

Piaget, Jean. *A Child's Conception of Physical Causality*. Translated by Marjorie Gabain. Totowa, NJ: Rowman & Littlefield, 1960.

―――― *The Child's Conception of the World*. Translated by Jean and Andrew Tomlinson. Totowa, NJ: Rowman & Littlefield, 1960.

―――― *The Construction of Reality in the Child*. Translated by Margaret Cook. New York: Ballantine Bks, 1971.

―――― *The Language and Thought of the Child*. Translated by Majorie Gabain. New York: World Pub (A Meridian Book), 1955.

―――― *Main Trends in Interdisciplinary Research*. New York: Harper & Row, 1973.

―――― *The Moral Judgment of the Child*. Translated by Marjorie Gabain. New York: Free Press, 1965.

―――― *Six Psychological Studies*. Translated by Anita Tenzer. New York: Vintage Bks, 1968.

CHILDHOOD—HISTORY OF

Ariès, Philippe. *Centuries of Childhood; A Social History of Family Life*. Translated by Robert Baldick. London: Cape, 1962.

169

BIBLIOGRAPHY

Bremner, Robert H., *et al.*, eds. *Children and Youth in America: A Documentary History.* 3 vols. Cambridge, MA: Harvard Univ. Press, 1970–71.
DeMause, Lloyd, ed. *History of Childhood.* New York: Psychohistory Press, 1974.

CHILDREN'S LIBERATION

Children's Rights; Toward the Liberation of the Child. Introduction by Paul Goodman. New York: Praeger, 1971.
Gottlieb, David, ed. *Children's Liberation.* Englewood Cliffs, NJ: Prentice-Hall, 1973.
Gross, Beatrice and Gross, Ronald. *The Children's Rights Movement: Overcoming the Oppression of Young People.* New York: Anchor Bks, 1977.
Holt, John. *Escape From Childhood: The Needs and Rights of Childhood.* New York: Ballantine Bks, 1975.
For current information on children's rights, libraries should subscribe to:
Children's Rights Report, American Civil Liberties Foundation, 22 East 40th Street, New York, NY 10016

CHILDREN'S LITERATURE

For everything you ever wanted to know about children's literature, its history and its criticism, consult:

Haviland, Virginia. *Children's Literature: A Guide to Reference Sources.* Washington, D.C.: Library of Congress, 1966. Supplement, 1972.
These two volumes provide critical evaluations of books about children's books, books about children's authors, international studies and much more. The two volumes are absolutely essential.
The following books have been published after the cut-off date for the Haviland Supplement. They are the ones I have found particularly useful.
Bettleheim, Bruno. *The Uses of Enchantment; The Meaning and Importance of Fairy Tales.* New York: Knopf, 1976.
Egoff, Sheila. *The Republic of Childhood; A Critical Guide to Canadian Children's Literature in English.* 2nd ed. Toronto: Oxford Univ. Press, 1975.
Haviland, Virginia. *Children and Literature; Views and Reviews.* Glenview, IL: Scott Foresman, 1973.

170

BIBLIOGRAPHY

Huck, Charlotte S. *Children's Literature in the Elementary School*. 3rd ed. New York: Holt, Rinehart & Winston, 1976.

Hürlimann, Bettina. *Picture-Book World*. Translated by Brian W. Alderson. Cleveland: World Pub, 1969.

Issues in Children's Book Selection; A School Library Journal/Library Journal Anthology. New York: Bowker, 1973.

Kingston, Carolyn T. *The Tragic Mode in Children's Literature*. New York: Teachers College Press, 1974.

Lanes, Selma G. *Down the Rabbit Hole; Adventures and Misadventures in the Realm of Children's Literature*. New York: Atheneum Pubs, 1971.

Larrick, Nancy. *A Parent's Guide to Children's Reading*. 4th ed. New York: Bantam Bks, 1975.

Lonsdale, Bernard J. and Mackintosh, Helen K. *Children Experience Literature*. New York: Random House, 1973.

Lukens, Rebecca J. *A Critical Handbook of Children's Literature*. Glenview, IL: Scott Foresman, 1976.

MacCann, Donnarae and Richard, Olga. *The Child's First Books; A Critical Study of Pictures and Texts*. New York: H. W. Wilson, 1973.

Notable Canadian Children's Books; Un choix de livres canadiens pour la jeunesse. "An annotated catalogue prepared by Sheila Egoff and Alvine Bélisle for an exhibition arranged by the National Library of Canada." Ottawa, Ontario: National Library of Canada, 1973.

Picture Books for Children. Edited by Patricia Jean Cianciolo. Chicago: American Library Association, 1973.

Ray, Sheila G. *Children's Fiction; A Handbook for Librarians*. Rev. ed. Leicester, England: Brockhampton Press, 1972.

Sebesta, Sam Leaton and Iverson, William J. *Literature for Thursday's Child*. Chicago: Science Research Associates, 1975.

Sutherland, Zena and Arbuthnot, May Hill. *Children and Books*. 5th ed. Glenview, IL: Scott Foresman, 1977.

Talent Is Not Enough; Mollie Hunter on Writing for Children. New York: Harper & Row, 1976.

CHILDREN'S SERVICE PROGRAMS

General

Barass, Reitel, and Associates, Inc. *A Study of Exemplary Public Library Reading and Reading Related Programs for Children, Youth, and Adults*. 2 vols. ERIC Document 066 197, July 1972.

Burke, J. Gordon and Shields, Gerald R. *Children's Library Service: School or Public?* Metuchen, NJ: Scarecrow Press, 1974.

Fleet, Anne. *Children's Libraries*. London: Deutch, 1973.
Gallivan, Marion F. "Research on Children's Services in Libraries: An Annotated Bibliography." *Top of the News*, April 1974, pp. 275–93.
Greenberg, Marilyn W. and Rothberg, Ryna H. "Don't Underrate Service to Children." *California Librarian*, April 1976, pp. 51–4.
Griffith, Ruth L. "A Library Sampling." *School Library Journal*, November 1974, p. 34.
Phinazee, Annette L. "The Early Childhood Library Specialist Program." *Journal of Education for Librarianship*, Winter 1976, pp. 183.
"Pillows, Quilts, and Soap Boxes." *School Library Journal*, February 1976, p. 31.
Polette, Nancy and Hamlin, Marjorie. *Reading Guidance in a Media Age*. Metuchen, NJ: Scarecrow Press, 1975.
Ray, Colin H. "Trends in Children's Librarianship." *UNESCO Bulletin for Libraries*, July 1974, pp. 188–92.
Shannon, Linda. "The Preschool Adventure Library." *School Library Journal*, November 1975, pp. 25–7.
Shockey, Annette, ed. "An *SLj* Symposium: Personalizing Library Service for Children and Young Adults." *School Library Journal*, March 1975, pp. 67–71.
Wilkins, Lea-Ruth C. "Kindergarten Children in the Library—It's Theirs Too!" *School Library Journal*, April 1975, pp. 28–30.

CHILDREN'S SERVICE PROGRAMS

Audiovisual Professional Aids

Investing in a Modern Miracle. This film focuses on the success a group of volunteers in Japan had in obtaining private financial support for children's library services and suggests American librarians should ask private enterprise for tax-deductible funds. For information, write: Westchester Library System, 280 North Central Avenue, Hartsdale, NY 10530.

The Pleasure Is Mutual. A classic film on the many forms the preschool program can take. From: Children's Book Council, 67 Irving Place, New York, NY 10003.

Prelude; Mini-Seminars on Using Books Creatively. Series 1 & 2. Six cassettes on storytelling, drama, poetry, etc. by well-known authorities. Uneven. From: Children's Book Council, 67 Irving Place, New York, NY 10003.

Stories in Motion. This film introduces "storytellers to alternative techniques to traditional storytelling." From: Audio-Visual Services Unit, Midstate Regional Library, RFD #4, Montpelier, VT 05602.

There's Something About a Story. Using a group of brand new storytellers, the film demonstrates the many ways a story can be told. From: Connecticut Films, Inc., 6 Cobble Hill Road, Westport, CT 06880.

Films, Music, and Toys

Artel, Linda and Wengraf, Susan E. "Programming Children's Films: Selection, Publicity, Evaluation." *Film Library Quarterly*, 7(3&4), 1974, pp. 50–60.

Bartle, F. R. "AV in the Children's Library?" *Australian Library Journal*, August 1974, pp. 247–52.

Crooks, Joyce M. "Classical Music for Children and Young Adults: A Discography." *School Library Journal*, November 1974, pp. 28–33.

Farrell, Diane. "Kaleidoscope—Programs for Children." *Horn Book*, February 1973, pp. 93–4.

Iarusso, Marilyn Berg. "Children's Films: Orphans of the Industry." *Film Library Quarterly*, 9(3), 1976, pp. 6–15.

Moll, Joy K. and Hermann, Patricia. "Evaluation and Selection of Toys, Games, and Puzzles." *Top of the News*, November 1974, pp. 86–9.

Moreland, Lesley. "Toytime Libraries." *Assistant Librarian*, April 1976, pp. 72–5.

Reid, M. T. "Houston Public Library's Toy Lending Library." *Texas Library Journal*, Summer 1975, pp. 82+.

"Toys and Games: The First Reading Tool." *School Library Journal*, April 1975, pp. 24–7.

"Toys for Loan." *School Library Journal*, April 1974, p. 14.

Puppetry

Crothers, J. Frances. *The Puppeteer's Library Guide, The Bibliographic Index to the Literature of the World Puppet Theatre.* Metuchen, NJ: Scarecrow Press, 1971.

Galvin, Mary. "Puppet Theater in Repertory." *Top of the News*, January 1975, pp. 220–4.

Hendrix, Margaret. "How a Simple Idea Has Mushroomed Into. . ." *Top of the News*, January 1975, p. 232.

Ransome, Grace Greenleaf. *Puppets and Shadows: A Bibliography.* Boston: Faxon Co., 1931. (Dated, but of interest to anyone wanting to specialize.)

Tharpe, Jac. "Recollections of a Puppet Maker." *Top of the News,* January 1975, pp. 233–6.

Wakefield, J. R. "Puppeting: An Alternate Expression." *California Librarian,* July 1975, pp. 40–5.

Young, Diana. "People, Puppets, and You." *Top of the News,* January 1975, pp. 218–19.

Storytelling

Chelton, Mary K. "Booktalking: You Can Do It." *School Library Journal,* April 1976, pp. 39–43.

Greene, Ellin. "The Preschool Story Hour Today." *Top of the News,* November 1974, pp. 80–5.

"Hear With Your Hands." *American Libraries,* December 1974, p. 597.

How to Conduct Effective Picture Book Programs: A Handbook. Compiled by Joanna Foster for use with the film, *The Pleasure Is Mutual.* Distributed by: Children's Book Council, 67 Irving Place, New York, NY 10003.

"I Gotta Make a Call: Dial-a-Story in Action." *School Library Journal,* October 1974, pp. 80–2.

Larrick, Nancy, "Poetry in the Story Hour." *Top of the News,* January 1976, pp. 151–61.

Sivulich, Kenneth G. and Sivulich, Sandra Stroner. "Media Library for Preschoolers; A Service of the Erie Metropolitan Library." *Top of the News,* November 1974, pp. 49–54.

Ziskind, Sylvia. *Telling Stories to Children.* New York: H. W. Wilson, 1976.

COLLECTION DEVELOPMENT

Bayer, Calvin J. *Book Selection Policies in American Libraries; An Anthology of Policies from College, Public, and School Libraries.* Austin, TX: Armadillo Press, 1973.

Carter, Mary Duncan and Bunk, Wally. *Building Library Collections.* 4th ed. Metuchen, NJ: Scarecrow Press, 1974. Chapter bibliographies are especially important.

CONTENT ANALYSIS

Berelson, Bernard. *Content Analysis in Communication Research.* Rev. ed. New York: Hafner Press, 1971.

Carney, Thomas F. *Content Analysis; A Technique for Systematic Inference from Communications.* London: Batsford, 1972.

Holsti, Ole R. *Content Analysis for the Social Sciences and Humanities.* Reading, MA: Addison-Wesley, 1969.

DEATH AND DYING

Easson, William M. *The Dying Child—The Management of the Child or Adolescent Who Is Dying.* Springfield, IL: Charles C. Thomas, 1970.

Grollman, Earl A. *Talking About Death.* Boston: Beacon Press, 1970.

Kastenbaum, Robert. "The Kingdom Where Nobody Dies." *Saturday Review/Science,* January 1973, pp. 33–8.

Kubler-Ross, Elisabeth. *On Death and Dying.* New York: Macmillan, 1969.

Mills, Gretchen C., *et. al. Discussing Death; A Guide to Death Education.* Homewood, IL: ETC Publns, 1976.

Reed, Elizabeth Liggett. *Helping Children With the Mystery of Death.* Nashville: Abingdon Press, 1970.

Wolf, Anna W. M. *Helping Your Child to Understand Death.* New York: Child Study Press, 1973.

Zim, Herbert S. and Bleeker, Sonia. *Life and Death.* New York: Morrow, 1970.

INTELLECTUAL FREEDOM

American Library Association. Office for Intellectual Freedom. *Intellectual Freedom Manual.* Chicago: American Library Association, 1974.

Berninghausen, David K. *The Flight From Reason; Essays on Intellectual Freedom in the Academy, the Press, and the Library.* Chicago: American Library Association, 1975.

Broderick, Dorothy M. "Racism, Sexism, Intellectual Freedom and Youth Librarians." *PLA Bulletin,* November 1976, pp. 122+.

Coughlan, Margaret. "Guardians of the Young. . ." *Top of the News,* Winter 1977, pp. 137–48.

Donelson, Ken. "Censorship in the 1970's; Some Ways to Handle It When It Comes (And It Will)." *English Journal,* February 1976, pp. 47–51.

Flanagan, Leo N. "Defending the Indefensible; The Limits of Intellectual Freedom." *Library Journal,* October 15, 1975, pp. 1887–91.

Geller, Evelyn. "The Librarian As Censor." *Library Journal,* June 1, 1976, pp. 1255–8.

——— "Somewhat Free: Post-Civil War Writing for Children." *Wilson Library Bulletin*, October 1976, pp. 172–6.

Issues in Children's Book Selection. New York: Bowker, 1973. Part II is devoted to "Intellectual Freedom or Censorship?"

Kanawha County, West Virginia: A Textbook Study in Cultural Conflict. Washington, DC: National Education Association, 1975.

Klein, Norma. "More Realism for Children." *Top of the News*, April 1975, pp. 307–12.

Kosinski. Jerzy. "Against Book Censorship." *Media and Methods*, January 1976, pp. 22–4.

Mazer, Norma Fox. "Comics, Cokes, & Censorship." *Top of the News*, January 1976, pp. 167–70.

Meyers, Duane H. "Boys and Girls and Sex and Libraries." *Library Journal*, February 15, 1977, pp. 457–463.

Newsletter on Intellectual Freedom. 6 issues per year. Chicago: American Library Association.

Page, Robert. "Holden Caulfield Is Alive and Well and Still Causing Trouble." *English Journal*, May 1975, pp. 27–31.

Raymond, Boris. "A Sword with Two Edges: The Role of Children's Literature in the Writings of N. K. Krupskaia." *Library Quarterly*, vol. 44, no. 3, pp. 206–18.

Serebnick, Judith. "The 1973 Court Rulings on Obscenity: Have They Made a Difference?" *Wilson Library Bulletin*, December 1975, pp. 304–10.

Williams, Patrick and Pearce, Jean Thornton. "Censorship Redefined." *Library Journal*, July 1976, pp. 1494–96.

Woodworth, Mary L. *Intellectual Freedom, the Young Adult, and Schools; A Wisconsin Study*. Madison, WI: Communication Programs, Univ. of Wisconsin—Extension, 1976.

INTERPERSONAL RELATIONS

Ginott, Haim G. *Between Parent & Child*. New York: Avon Bks, 1965.

Gordon, Thomas. *P.E.T. Parent Effectiveness Training; The Tested New Way to Raise Responsible Children*. New York: New Am. Lib, 1975.

Harris, Thomas A. *I'm OK—You're OK*. New York: Avon Bks, 1973.

Samples, Bob and Wohlford, Bob. *Opening: A Primer for Self-Actualization*. Reading, MA: Addison-Wesley, 1975.

For an analysis of the major parent-training courses currently popular:

Brown, Catherine Caldwell. "It Changed My Life." *Psychology Today*, November 1976, pp. 47+.

BIBLIOGRAPHY

NON-LIBRARY PERIODICALS

The following periodicals are those I find most useful in helping me keep up with research in child development, racism, and sexism awareness studies, and content analyses of the media.

Journal of Abnormal Child Psychology. Quarterly. V. H. Winston & Co. 1511 K Street, N.W., Washington, DC 20005.

Journal of Abnormal Psychology. Bi-monthly. American Psychological Association, 1200 17th Street, N.W., Washington, DC 20036.

Journal of Communication. Quarterly. P.O. Box 13358, Philadelphia, PA 19101.

Journal of Moral Education. 3 times per year. NFER Publishing Company Ltd., 2, Jennings Buildings, Thames Avenue, Windsor, Berks SL4 1QS, England.

Journal of Personality and Social Psychology. Quarterly. American Psychological Association. 1200 17th Street, N.W., Washington, DC 20036.

Journal of Popular Culture. Quarterly. University Hall, Bowling Green University, Bowling Green, OH 43403.

Journal of Social Psychology. Quarterly. 2 Commercial Street, Provincetown, MA 02657.

RACISM AND SEXISM

The Acorn Groweth . . . Resources on Sexism in Library Materials for Children and Young Adults. 3 times per year. Rita Kort, 48 Sunset Ave., Venice, CA 90291.

Akwesasne Notes. Mohawk Nation, via Rooseveltown, NY 13683. Important for news and views of the status of native people; also lists numerous resources in all media.

Altemeyer, Robert A. and Jones, Keith. "Sexual Identity, Physical Attractiveness and Seating Position As Determinants of Influence in Discussion Groups." *Canadian Journal of Behavioural Science*, October 1974, pp. 357–75.

Asia in American Textbooks. New York: Asia Society, Inc., n.d.

Bardwick, Judith M. and Douvan, Elizabeth. "Ambivalence: The Socialization of Women." In Gornick, Vivian and Moran, Barbara K., eds. *Woman in Sexist Society.* New York: Basic Bks, 1971. (Also an NAL pb.)

Bem, Sandra Lipsitz. "Androgyny Vs. the Tight Little Lives of Fluffy Women and Chesty Men." *Psychology Today*, September 1975, pp. 58–62.

Books for the Multi-Racial Classroom; A Select List of Children's Books Showing the Backgrounds of India, Pakistan and the West Indies. Pamphlet Number Ten. Birmingham, England: The Library Association Youth Libraries Group, 1971.

Broderick, Dorothy M. *Image of the Black in Children's Fiction.* New York: Bowker, 1973.

Broverman, Inge K., *et al.* "Sex-Role Stereotyping and Clinical Judgments of Mental Health." *Journal of Consulting and Clinical Psychology,* 1970, 34, pp. 1–7.

Channeling Children: Sex Stereotyping in Prime-Time TV. Princeton, NJ: Women on Words and Images, 1975.

Clark, Kenneth B. and Clark, M. P. "Racial Identification and Preference in Negro Children." In Society for the Psychological Study of Social Issues. *Readings in Social Psychology.* New York: Holt, 1947.

Coles, Robert. *Children of Crisis: A Study of Courage and Fear.* New York: Delta, 1968. See particularly Chapter 3, "When I Draw the Lord He'll Be A Real Big Man."

Dick and Jane As Victims; Sex Stereotyping in Children's Readers. Princeton, NJ: Women on Words and Images, 1972.

Freeman, Jo. "The Building of the Gilded Cage." In Koedt, Anne, *et al.*, eds. *Radical Feminism.* New York: Quadrangle, 1973.

Gersoni, Diane. *Sexism and Youth.* New York: Bowker, 1974.

Goldberg, Phillip A. "Are Women Prejudiced Against Women?" *Transaction,* 5, 1968, pp. 28–30.

Goodman, Mary Ellen. *Race Awareness in Young Children.* New York: Collier Bks, 1964 [c. 1952].

Grier, William H. and Cobbs, Price M. *Black Rage.* New York: Basic Bks, 1968.

Guideline for Improving the Image of Women in Textbooks. Glenview, IL: Scott Foresman, 1972.

Guidelines for Equal Treatment of the Sexes in McGraw-Hill Publications. New York: McGraw-Hill Public Information and Publicity Department, n.d.

Heshusius-Gilsdorf, Lous T. and Gilsdorf, Dale L. "Girls Are Females, Boys Are Males; A Content Analysis of Career Materials." *Personnel and Guidance Journal,* December 1975, pp. 207–11. Has excellent bibliography on sex-role stereotyping.

Interracial Books for Children Bulletin. Council on Interracial Books of Children, Inc. 1841 Broadway, New York, NY 10023.

178

Jensen, Arthur R. "How Much Can We Boost I.Q. and Scholastic Achievement?" *Harvard Educational Review,* Winter, 1969, pp. 1–123.

Kelty, Jean McClure. "The Cult of Kill in Adolescent Fiction." *English Journal,* February 1975, pp. 56+.

Kinloch, Graham C. *The Dynamics of Race Relations; A Sociological Analysis.* New York: McGraw-Hill, 1974.

Lambert, Wallace E. and Klineberg, Otto. *Children's Views of Foreign People.* New York: Appleton-Century-Crofts, 1967.

Lasker, Bruno. *Race Attitudes in Children.* New York: Greenwood Press, 1968. A reprint of the 1929 landmark study.

MacCann, Donnarae and Woodard, Gloria. *Black America in Books for Children: Readings in Racism.* Metuchen, NJ: Scarecrow Press, 1972.

McDiarmid, Garnet and Pratt, David. *Teaching Prejudice.* Toronto, Ontario: Ontario Institute for Studies in Education, 1971.

Nelson, Gayle. "The Double Standard in Adolescent Novels." *English Journal,* February 1975, pp. 53+.

Porter, Judith D. R. *Black Child, White Child; The Development of Racial Attitudes.* Cambridge, MA: Harvard Univ. Press, 1971.

Reading, Children's Books, and Our Pluralistic Society. Compiled and edited by Harold Tanyzer and Jean Karl. Newark, DE. International Reading Association, 1972.

Richardson, Ken, *et al.,* eds. *Race and Intelligence: The Fallacies Behind the Race-IQ Controversy.* Baltimore: Penguin Bks, 1972.

Shockley, William. "Dysgenics, Geneticity, Racelogy: A Challenge to the Intellectual Responsibility of Educators." *Phi Delta Kappan,* January 1972, pp. 297–307.

Slater, Philip. *The Pursuit of Loneliness; American Culture at the Breaking Point.* Boston: Beacon Press, 1970. See particularly Chapter 3, "Women and Children First."

Stanford, Barbara and Stanford, Gene. *Roles & Relationships; A Practical Guide to Teaching About Masculinity and Femininity.* New York: Bantam Bks, 1976.

Textbooks and the American Indian. The Indian Historian Press, Inc. 1451 Masonic Avenue, San Francisco, CA 94117.

Weisstein, Naomi. "Psychology Constructs the Female." In Gornick, Vivian and Moran, Barbara K., eds. *Woman in Sexist Society.* New York: Basic Bks, 1971.

SEX EDUCATION

Bernstein, Anne C. "How Children Learn About Sex and Birth." *Psychology Today*, Janurary 1976, pp. 31+.

Boston Women's Health Book Collective. *Our Bodies, Ourselves*. Rev. ed. New York: Simon & Schuster, 1976.

ED-U Press. 760 Ostrom Avenue, Syracuse, NY 13210.

All libraries should be on the mailing list for ED-U Press since it consistently produces publications of major importance.

Laycock, S. R. *Family Living and Sex Education*. Published for Canadian Health Education Specialists Society, Ottawa. Toronto, Ontario: Mil-Mac Publns.

Miller, Mary Susan and Schiller, Patricia. *A Teachers' Round Table on Sex Education*. Boston: National Association of Independent Schools, 1977.

Contains the results of a survey of sex education programs in private schools, articles on why offer the courses, sample curricula, and bibliography. *Vital*.

Resource Catalogue; Booklets, Posters, Films, Family Planning, Sex Education, Population. Compiled and distributed by Planned Parenthood Federation. Available free from local offices upon request.

Sex Education at Home. Available from: Community Sex Education Center of Planned Parenthood Center, 1120 East Genesee Street, Syracuse, NY 13210.

Sex News; A Monthly Digest of News, Views, Events, Publications and Resources. Edited by P. K. Houdek, 7140 Oak, Kansas City, MO 64114.

Title accurately describes the scope of its contents. Important tool.

Sexuality and Human Values; The Personal Dimension of Sexual Experience. Edited by Mary S. Calderone. New York: Association Press, (A Siecus Book), 1974.

SELECTION TOOLS

Bibliographic Aids

Alternatives in Print 75–76; A Catalog of Social Change Publications. Compiled by SRRT (ALA) Task Force on AIP. San Francisco: Glide Publications, 1975.

Children's Books in Print. New York: Bowker, annual.

Paperback Books in Print. New York: Bowker, annual.

Subject Guide to Children's Books in Print. New York: Bowker, annual.

Current and Selective

AAAS Science Book List for Children. 3rd ed. Compiled by Hilary J. Deason. Washington, DC: American Association for the Advancement of Science, 1972.

Appraisal, Children's Science Books. 3 times per year. Longfellow Hall, 13 Appian Way, Cambridge, MA 02138.

Best Books for Children. Compiled by the editors of *School Library Journal.* New York: Bowker, annual.

Best in Children's Books; the University of Chicago Guide to Children's Literature, 1966–1972. Chicago: Univ. of Chicago Press, 1973.

Bilingual Bicultural Materials; A Listing for Library Resource Centers. El Paso, TX: Board of Education, El Paso Public Schools, 1974.

Booklist. Twice monthly, September–July and once in August. Chicago: American Library Association.

Bulletin of the Center for Children's Books. Monthly except August. Chicago: Univ. of Chicago Press.

Canadian Materials. 3 times per year. Box 190, Station O, Toronto, Ontario M4A 2N3.

Children's Book Review Service, Inc. Twelve monthly issues, plus fall and spring special supplements. 220 Berkeley Place, #1D, Brooklyn, NY 11217.

Children's Books of the Year. Selected and annotated by Elaine Moss. London: Hamish Hamilton Children's Books Ltd., annual.

Children's Catalog. New York: H. W. Wilson Co. Compilation every five years with annual supplements.

Elementary School Library Collection. Newark, NJ: Bro-Dart Foundation, annual.

Emergency Librarian. Bi-monthly. Subscriptions to: Barbara Clubb, 697 Wellington Crescent, Winnipeg, Manitoba R3M OA7.

Horn Book. Bi-monthly. 585 Boylston Street, Boston, MA 02116.

In Review. Quarterly. Provincial Library Service, 14th Floor, Mowat Block, Toronto, Ontario M7A 1C5.

Junior High School Catalog. New York: H. W. Wilson Co. Compilation every five years with annual supplements.

Language Arts. (formerly *Elementary English*). September–May. National Council of Teachers of English, 1111 Kenyon Road, Urbana, IL 61801.

Media & Methods. September–May. North American Publishing Co., 401 N. Broad Street, Philadelphia, PA 19108.

Positive Images; A Guide to Non-Sexist Films for Young People. San Francisco: Booklegger Press, 1976.

181

Previews. September–May. R. R. Bowker, 1180 Avenue of the Americas, New York, NY 10036.

Reading Teacher. 8 times per year. International Reading Association, 800 Barksdale Road, Newark, DE 19711.

School Library Journal. September–May. R. R. Bowker, 1180 Avenue of the Americas, New York, NY 10036.

Science and Children. 8 times per year. National Science Teachers Association, 1742 Connecticut Avenue, N.W. Washington, DC 20009.

Social Education. October–May, except November/December combined. National Council for the Social Studies, 1515 Wilson Blvd., Suite 101, Arlington, VA 22209.

Words Like Freedom; A Multi-Cultural Bibliography. Compiled by the Human Relations Committee. Burlingame, CA: California Association of School Librarians, 1975.

TELEVISION

For excellent commentary and bibliographies on children and television:

Breslin, Deirdre and Marino, Eileen. "Television: Its Impact and Influence." In Sutherland, Zena and Arbuthnot, May Hill. *Children and Books.* 5th ed. Glenview, IL: Scott, 1977, pp. 596–602.

Liebert, Robert M. *Television and Children; A Psychology Today Cassette Interview.* From *Psychology Today,* Consumer Service Division, 595 Broadway, New York, NY 10012.

Stein, Aletha Huston and Friedrich, Lynette Kohn. "Impact of Television on Children and Youth." In *Review of Child Development Research,* vol. 5. Chicago: Univ. of Chicago Press, 1975, pp. 183–256.

Audiovisual Sources

Here are a few of the producers and distributors of films, filmstrips, and phonodiscs/cassettes about children's literature. All libraries should be on the mailing lists for catalogs and promotional materials. *Previews* is an excellent source for additional distributors.

Caedmon, 505 8th Avenue, New York, NY 10018.

Guidance Associates, 757 Third Avenue, New York, NY 10017.

Jabberwocky, Box 6727, San Francisco, CA 94101.

Magic Circle, distributed by Xerox Films, 245 Long Hill Road, Middletown, CT 06457.

Miller-Brody Productions, 342 Madison Avenue, New York, NY 10017.

Society for Visual Education, 1345 Diversey Parkway, Chicago, IL 60614.

Weston Woods, Weston, CT 06880.

Libraries should also hold membership in:

Educational Film Library Association, 17 W. 60th Street, New York, NY 10023.

Children's Books Mentioned in the Text

The following books were cited in the text. This is not a recommended buying list.

Andry, Andrew C. and Shepp, Steven. *How Babies Are Made.* Illustrations by Blake Hampton. New York: Time-Life, 1968.

Appleton, Victor. *Tom Swift Jr. and the Cosmic Astronauts.* New York: Grosset & Dunlap, 1960.

Atwater, Richard. *Mr. Popper's Penquins.* Illustrations by Robert Lawson. Boston: Little, Brown, 1938.

Baum, L. Frank. *The Wizard of Oz.* Illustrations by W. W. Denslow. Chicago: Reilly, 1956. (First published in 1900.)

Blume, Judy. *Are You There God? It's Me, Margaret.* Scarsdale: Bradbury, 1970.

——— *It's Not the End of the World.* Scarsdale: Bradbury, 1972.

Buck, Pearl. *Johnny Jack and His Beginnings.* New York: John Day, 1954.

Carroll, Lewis. *Alice's Adventures in Wonderland.* See *Children's Catalog* for recommended editions.

Childress, Alice. *A Hero Ain't Nothing But a Sandwich.* New York: Coward, 1973.

Dixon, Paige. *May I Cross Your Golden River?* New York: Atheneum, 1975.

Ets, Marie Hall. *Nine Days to Christmas.* New York: Viking, 1959.

——— *The Story of a Baby.* New York: Viking, 1939.

Finley, Martha. *Elsie Dinsmore.* New York: Grosset & Dunlap, n.d. (First published in 1867.)

Fitzhugh, Louise. *Harriet the Spy.* New York: Harper, 1964.

——— *The Long Secret.* New York: Harper, 1965.

Flack, Marjorie. *The Story About Ping.* Illustrations by Kurt Wiese. New York: Viking, 1933.

Forbes, Esther. *Johnny Tremain.* Boston: Houghton Mifflin, 1943.

Gág, Wanda. *Millions of Cats.* New York: Coward, 1928.

Goudey, Alice. *Houses from the Sea.* Illustrations by Adrienne Adams. New York: Scribner's, 1959.

Grahame, Kenneth. *Wind in the Willows.* Illustrations by Ernest H. Shepard. New York: Scribner's, 1953. (First published in 1903.)

Greene, Betty. *Summer of My German Soldier.* Dial, New York: 1973.

Gunther, John. *Death Be Not Proud.* New York: Harper, 1949.

Hegeler, Sten. *Peter and Caroline: A Child Asks About Childbirth and*

184

Sex. Translated by Maurice Michael. London: Tavistock Publications, 1957.

Hogben, Lancelot. *The Wonderful World of Mathematics.* Illustrations by Andre, Charles Keeping, Kenneth Symonds. Rev. ed. Garden City, NY: Doubleday, 1968.

Kellogg, Marjorie. *Like the Lion's Tooth.* New York: Farrar, Straus and Giroux, 1972.

Kennedy, Richard. *Come Again in the Spring.* Illustrations by Marcia Sewall. New York: Harper, 1976.

Kingsley, Charles. *Water Babies.* New York: Dutton, n.d. (First published in 1863.)

Klein, Norma. *Mom, the Wolfman and Me.* New York: Pantheon, 1972.

Lindgren, Astrid. *Pippi Longstocking.* Translated by Florence Lamborn. Illustrations by Louis Glanzman. New York: Viking, 1950.

Lund, Doris. *Eric.* Philadelphia: Lippincott, 1974.

McBride, Will. *Show Me! A Picture Book of Sex for Children and Parents.* New York: St. Martin's, 1975.

McCloskey, Robert. *Make Way for Ducklings.* New York: Viking, 1941.

Mayle, Peter. *"Where Did I Come From?"* Illustrations by Arthur Robins. New York: Lyle Stuart, 1973.

Neufeld, John. *Freddy's Book.* New York: Random House, 1973.

Peck, Richard. *Are You in the House Alone?* New York: Viking, 1976.

———— *Dreamland Lake.* New York: Holt, 1973.

Platt, Kin. *Headman.* New York: Greenwillow Bks, 1975.

Pomeroy, Wardell B. *Boys and Sex.* New York: Delacorte, 1968.

———— *Girls and Sex.* New York: Delacorte, 1969.

Rey, H. A. *Curious George Rides a Bike.* Boston: Houghton Mifflin, 1952.

Sandoz, Mari. *The Horsecatcher.* Philadelphia: Westminster, 1957.

Scott's Specialized Catalog of United States Stamps. New York: Scott. Issued periodically.

Shecter, Ben. *Across the Meadow.* Garden City, NY: Doubleday, 1973.

Steptoe, John. *My Special Best Words.* New York: Viking, 1974.

Swift, Jonathan. *Gulliver's Travels.* See *Children's Catalog* for recommended editions.

White, E. B. *Charlotte's Web.* Illustrations by Garth Williams. New York: Harper, 1952.

———— *Stuart Little.* Illustrations by Garth Williams. New York: Harper, 1945.

Index